CRAVEABLE

SEEMA PANKHANIA

CRAVEABLE

Photography by Haarala Hamilton

MICHAEL JOSEPH

For my mum,
the strongest woman in my life,
I owe everything to you

ALL I WANT TO EAT IS …

1 SOMETHING FRESH [25]

2 SOMETHING SALTY & SAVOURY [53]

3 SOMETHING SPICY [79]

4 SOMETHING GREEN [103]

5 SOMETHING COMFORTING [125]

6 SOMETHING SPECIAL [157]

7 SOMETHING SWEET [191]

8 SOMETHING NOW! [219]

WELCOME TO CRAVEABLE

Every day most of my thoughts are consumed with what I'm going to eat next. Literally every waking moment. If I'm not thinking about food, I'm asking my friends what they ate for breakfast, aimlessly strolling through supermarkets or just scrolling through endless dishes on social media.

And since I think about food all day, when I'm hungry and need to cook, I've become very good at making dishes that specifically suit for my cravings, which is kind of how this book was created.

I want this book to be a collection of simple (or simple enough!) trusted recipes that you can turn to, to take some of the decision making out of your day – for when you need something spicy, salty, sweet, fresh, or just need to make a quick meal that's still delicious. It may be that it's super warm outside and you want something bright and fresh; perhaps you're bored at your desk and need something spicy to perk you up, or maybe you're just feeling like you need something cozy and comforting after a long cold day.

As someone who usually shares their recipes on TikTok and Instagram, having them all written down in a book is so fantastic. Believe me, I know the faff of watching something online, pausing and scrawling down notes to try and replicate it at home, and never quite knowing if you're doing it right. I also really love flicking through books for inspiration and knowing that they are more vigorously tested than a random recipe online, and hope this book can be that for you!

As much as I might like to be, I'm not a planner, especially when it comes to food. I understand and admire those who can meal prep, but the joy for me is creating something that just really fits for what I need in that exact moment – I never really know what I'm going to eat in the evening on the morning of that same day, let alone the weekend before! It's just not how I cook. And though the world is always telling us that we should be meal prepping, batch cooking and generally filling our fridges with as much food as possible, the 30 minutes that I spend at the end of each day making myself something delicious is as satisfying as it gets for me. Because of this, most of the recipes in this book use simple ingredients that you might already have at home or, if not, can easily be picked up from your local corner shop. Where slightly harder-to-find ingredients have been used, I have always tried to list a simple substitute that can be used without impacting the end result. There is also a full list of simple subs on pages 22–23.

Saying that, I don't want you to feel scared of using what you've already got in the cupboard instead, or changing things up to make the recipes feel like your own. Be brave and adjust things to your taste and enjoy the journey along the way – just don't forget to taste as you go!

Above all, this book is yours and I hope that you turn to it time and again on those days when you just can't figure out what to cook. Fold the pages, write in the margins, spatter the recipes with sauce and, most of all, enjoy!

Seema x

HOW I REALLY
GOT INTO COOKING

(AND SOME MORE BITS FOR ALL YOU NOSY PEOPLE OUT THERE)

As you can imagine, food has always been incredibly important to me – and if you ever had the chance to visit my mum's house, you would see exactly where that comes from! Food was the thing that always tied our family together. My mum made a fresh meal from scratch every single day: we never ate out, we never had takeaway or oven food, we never ate in front of the TV. But at 7pm every day, my family would gather around the dining table in our house in Slough. Prior to those mealtimes, me and my brother would often hover in the kitchen so that the rotli could come fresh out of the thava (cast iron pan) and straight into our mouths. Usually, our meals were made up of some kind of curry, a dal, some pickles my mum had smuggled in her suitcase from India, papar (also known as poppadoms) and freshly made rotli with rice to follow. Looking back now, it really was a feast to be eating like this, especially when my mum was doing this every day whilst also juggling two jobs and two kids. I didn't appreciate it at the time, but I find it astonishing looking back at it now. She didn't have a big budget but somehow managed to create all of this absolutely delicious food, and I think that's something that's inspired me in my cooking, and hopefully something you'll see through the recipes in this book. Great food isn't about having hundreds of ingredients, it's about how you use the ingredients that you do have. In this way, my mum's cooking was what made me first fall in love with food, and so many of her dishes are still my go-to when I want something comforting. Making

her Pea & Potato Curry (see page 146) or her 10-Minute Emergency Dal (see page 242) is what real comfort food is for me.

My mum pretty much only made Indian food at home so that's what I ate every day growing up, but I was desperate to learn more about different foods from around the world. This took off in a major way when I ended up having to take a year off school after being diagnosed with cancer at age 13. It sounds much sadder than it was (or as I saw it at the time) – I wasn't really old enough to understand the severity of it all and, for me, it mainly meant that I got a lot of time off school to watch daytime TV, specifically the cooking channels! My mum made sure that I was able to fuel my new-found love by buying second-hand cooking equipment from car-boot sales and from eBay. (As a side note, I still get my cake tins from car-boot sales now and recommend you do the same – you can get great-quality, barely used tins for about 50p!). I ended up spending a year at home watching TV and baking to my heart's content, and by the time I was well enough to return to school, I was baking all my friends' birthday cakes (ones that looked like teddy bears and penguins) and even selling a few on Facebook!

I returned to school, now considering a career in food, but when it came down to picking my A-levels, a bit of research told me that culinary school would cost me about £50K upfront (which I obviously did not

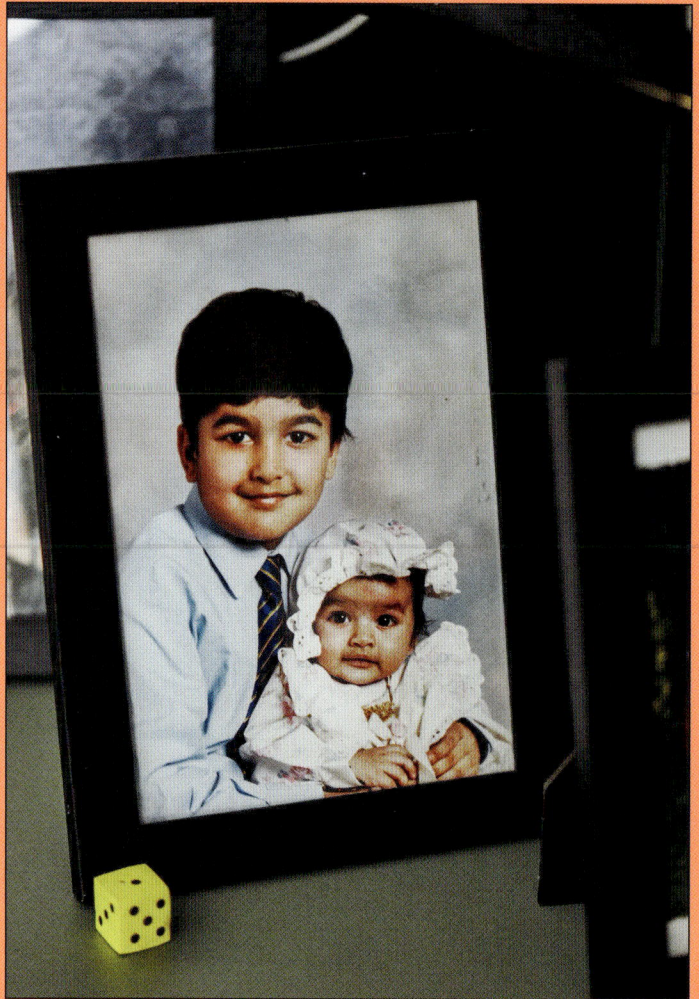

Me and my older brother Hitesh.

have), and getting a degree at a good Uni seemed the more sensible choice. I studied at Manchester University, achieving a pretty good neuroscience degree, and throughout it all I cooked and learned as much as I could about food. Where I studied was next to a fantastically stocked East Asian supermarket, and though I had very little knowledge of East Asian food, I would trawl the aisles for new and exciting ingredients and bring them home to experiment, looking up recipes on YouTube and trying to replicate them myself.

On one of those nights I wanted to learn how to make a Filipino dish, since I had never tried any nor thought I would be able to visit the Philippines any time soon. Chicken adobo, the national dish of the Philippines, is chicken cooked with a cup of white vinegar and a cup of soy sauce. As you can imagine the entire uni flat reeked of vinegar and my flat mates who were just about to leave for a night out were fuming. But when the chicken simmered down, the vinegar tenderised the meat and the soy melded with the flavours and made it incredibly savoury – it was one of the nicest meals I had ever made and none of us had ever heard of it before. I was so amazed at how simple it was and slightly angry that more people didn't know about it. I wanted to learn more dishes like this from around the world, simple home-cooked dishes that anyone can make but are just a little less known - and that's how I started making every country's national dish.

As I was approaching graduation, I knew I didn't want a career in neuroscience or to be stuck in an office job in London. So I thought I'd give myself a year to try working in restaurants, and if, worst-case scenario, I hated it, I'd still be able to apply for grad schemes afterwards. I was already sharing a few photos on my Instagram, and had gained a moderate following of just less than 2,000 (using the good ol' follow-and-unfollow technique) so I reached out to a few chefs that I admired to ask for advice. Only one (my favourite one) replied, Ravneet Gill. Rav invited me for a day to shadow her in the restaurant she was working at. Being an Indian girl who wanted to get into cooking, seeing any representation was close to nil, so seeing her succeed and have my dream job was so inspiring. Over the day she told me to forget all about cookery school (thank God! as where was I meant to get £50K from?!) and to get into a professional kitchen as soon as I could instead. So that's what I did.

The week I graduated from university I set up five trial shifts at different restaurants in London, leaving my top pick, Gordon Ramsay's Lucky Cat, for the final day. As the week went on, I got to know a bit about how restaurant kitchens work and what was expected of me, so on that final shift I was ready to try and make a stellar impression. I was offered a job the same day, and somehow was now a professional chef – it must have been the unwavering excitement of being in a kitchen that got me through.

The thing about working in restaurant kitchens is that the hours are horrendous. I was starting work at 8 am and would get home at 1 am; my mum would greet me at the door with a bucket of salted hot water to soak my legs and relax my muscles. Then she would give me a big glass of warm milk with honey and send me to bed, just so I could get up in the morning and do it again the next day. I did that for almost two years, everyday riding my moped in from Slough to London.

It was exhausting, but though there were days when I almost couldn't bear to get on that moped and head off to work, I always did because I knew that working in the restaurant and learning all these new skills was going to open so many doors into a career I loved. Then one day the long hours caught up with me when I was riding to work in the rain, exhausted from a week of long shifts and probably not paying quite as much attention as I should have been. The car in front of me indicated right but I missed his signal and ended up crashing into the back of it as it turned a corner. I was actually pretty hurt and ended up being bundled into the back of an ambulance, but all I remember from that moment was the feeling of relief that I wasn't going to be able to go into the restaurant that day.

I took some time off to mend my fractured elbow and during that time MOB kitchen posted an application for an on-screen chef. By a strange stroke of luck, since I wasn't working 16-hour shifts, I was able to apply for the job, with the help of my brother and his girlfriend (now wife!). We created the most silly and ridiculous job application we could. I didn't end up getting that role, but I left the job in the kitchen and I started a side business selling brownies and doughnuts from my mum's house in Slough whilst I looked for work. The brownies were booming. I spent weeks testing out recipes to get the perfect brownie and ended up shipping them all over the country. I'm very proud of that brownie recipe and you can find it on page 193.

During this stage, MOB called me up out of the blue, saying they remembered my silly video and wanted to offer me a role – as long as I was able to start the following Monday! Luckily (again!) I didn't have a job and so took up the offer immediately. I remember so vividly me and my brother squealing as soon as I got off the phone to Sophie Wyburd.

I had the best time working for MOB and loved being in that fun, creative environment with such talented people every day. I was able to spend my time learning about food and social media, and just really let my obsession for food take over – and all that with some of my favourite people I've met alongside me, it really was a dream job. It wasn't until Jake Gauntlett really pushed me to make my own videos for the national dish series, which I had kept in my head since I first made that chicken adobo at uni, that it all really took off. I soon wanted to create more videos for my own page and have full creative freedom on them, so I took the leap and left MOB but still very much kept all of the friendships I made there with me.

Now I get the privilege of being able to cook and create to my heart's content, trying out different styles of content, travelling to learn more about food and keeping you all along on this journey with me. Whether you were one of those first 2,000 followers or if you're just joining me now, thank you so much for reading this far and all the support you give. I really hope you enjoy this book. Social media can be a weird and scary place, but it can lead to some pretty special things.

WHAT ARE YOU CRAVING?

The way that I face the issue of what to eat for dinner usually just depends on what I'm craving in that exact moment. If it's a beautifully hot day then I'm most likely to want something fresh, but if I'm nursing a brutal hangover then I probably just need something (anything!) right now! So that's what I decided this book should be, a collection of recipes that suited every mood and craving. In doing so, I found that most of my moods and the cravings that matched them could be broken down into the following categories:

All I want to eat is something ───────────────────────────fresh

All I want to eat is something ──────────────────────salty & savoury

All I want to eat is something ────────────────────────spicy

All I want to eat is something ────────────────────────green

All I want to eat is something ──────────────────────comforting

All I want to eat is something ────────────────────────special

All I want to eat is something ────────────────────────sweet

All I want to eat is something ────────────────────────NOW!

And so that is how I have ordered this book. For the most part the recipes are simple and can easily be made on a Tuesday night after work with perhaps just a quick trip to your local shop on the way home for the handful of ingredients that you don't already have to hand, though some are more labour intensive. The something special chapter (pages 157–89) is for those times when you've got friends or family over and you want a project. For me, that time spent over the stove prepping a meal is itself a craving. I love those minutes and hours spent creating something fantastic that you know your guests will love. The something NOW! chapter (pages 219–43) is the very opposite of that. These are my emergency recipes. They are generally meals for one, for when you're in a mad rush, perhaps feeling jaded and in need of an immediate pick-me-up that might otherwise come in the form of an expensive takeaway. I've put them at the back of the book, after even the desserts, so you have immediate access when then need arises.

My criteria for desserts is that they have to be show stopping and deliciously moreish, and I've created a whole chapter for you in this book. They are what turn occasions into something a bit more special. Just try and eat a Caramelized Banana Split (page 212) or take a bite of a Tangfastic Doughnut (page 194) and not have a smile on your face afterwards.

I hope that ordering the recipes in this way makes as much sense to you as it does to me, but I'm also treating you to a slightly more traditional recipe list on the next page, just in case you do, in fact, simply want to find the dinner recipes.

A RECIPE LIST
(THE TRADITIONAL WAY)

MEATY MAINS

SWEET DISHES

FIND YOUR OWN
SPICE LEVEL

MILD　　　　　　　　　　　　　　　　　　　　MEDIUM

1　　　　　　　　2　　　　　　　　3

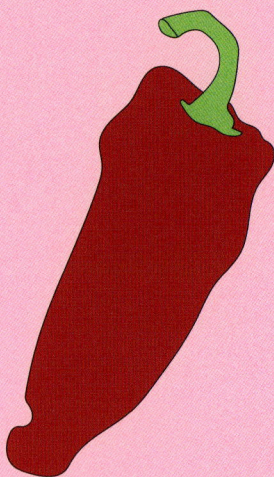

Green (serrano) chilli

Ancho chillies　　　Jalapeños

Red (serrano) chilli　　Green finger chillies

20

I've always thought that I had a pretty high tolerance for heat, a fact that I confidently repeated to a street-food vendor on a trip to Thailand before being put firmly in my place as to what 'spicy' actually was. Mouth burning and eyes watering, I had to come to terms with the fact that I do have a limit, and so do you. I like spicy food (there's a whole chapter in this book!) and the recipes that use chilli in this book do tend to pack a punch, but the beauty of making anything from scratch is that you can tailor it to your tastes. Feel free to reduce, omit or even double-up on the chilli in these recipes. Find your own spice level. To help you get there, I've designed a table to give you a bit more info about the spice levels of the different chillies used in this book below. If you're eyeing up a recipe with a Scotch bonnet and think you might find the heat too much, swap in whatever other chilli you have to hand that better suits your spice preference.

MEDIUM   HOT

3   4   5

Thai red (bird's-eye) chilli

Habanero chilli

Long red (cayenne) chillies

Scotch bonnet chilli

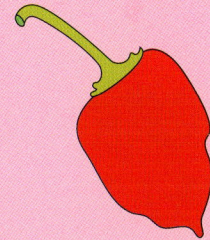

NOTE

→ *Chillies store brilliantly in the freezer! I don't always get through fresh chillies fast enough, so store any extras in the freezer for whenever they are needed. No need to defrost, just use straight from frozen!*

SIMPLE
SUBSTITUTIONS

INGREDIENT		SUGGESTED SUBSTITUTIONS
Amchoor Powder	↔	Sumac or Lime Zest
Ancho Chillies	↔	Dried Chipotles or Guajillos
Anchovies	↔	Miso, Marmite, Parmesan, Chopped Bacon
Apple Cider Vinegar	↔	Sherry or White Wine Vinegar
Bird's-Eye Chilli	↔	Long Red Chilli (Amount Halved)
Black Chinese Vinegar	↔	Balsamic Vinegar
Chives	↔	Spring Onions
Chorizo	↔	N'duja or Other Spicy Sausage
Coconut Oil	↔	Vegetable Oil
Coconut Yoghurt	↔	Plain Yoghurt
Coriander Seeds	↔	Cumin Seeds
Crème Fraîche	↔	Sour Cream or Yoghurt
Dried Tarragon	↔	Dried Sage or Oregano
Dried Thyme	↔	Dried Rosemary
Fennel Seeds	↔	Cumin Seeds
Ghee	↔	Butter
Gherkins	↔	Pickles or Cornichons
Green Chillies	↔	Jalapeño Chillies
Green Lentils	↔	Red Split Lentils

I'm a firm believer in using the ingredients that you already have rather than having to spend precious time and money getting hold of special ingredients, and I want you to be the same when making the recipes from this book. If you come across an ingredient that you don't recognize or that you just can't be bothered to trek to the shops for, give this list a scan and see if you can find it and its recommended substitute here. I've also listed these individually on the recipes themselves, but thought it would be useful to have them all in one place.

INGREDIENT		SUGGESTED SUBSTITUTIONS
Hoisin	↔	Honey
Nutritional Yeast	↔	Parmesan (or Any Hard Cheese), Grated
Parmesan	↔	Any Hard Cheese
Peanut Butter	↔	Any Nut Butter
Peanuts	↔	Cashews, Almonds or Macadamias
Pretzels (Sweet Dishes)	↔	Digestive Biscuits
Radishes	↔	Celery
Red Onions	↔	White Onions
Rice Vinegar	↔	White Wine Vinegar or Apple Cider Vinegar
Shallots	↔	Onions (Amount Halved)
Shaoxing Wine	↔	Dry Sherry, White Wine or Mirin
Soft Dark Brown Sugar	↔	Soft Light Brown Sugar
Sour Cream	↔	Yoghurt
Sriracha	↔	Any Other Chilli Sauce
Sumac	↔	Combo of ½ Za'atar, ½ Sesame Seeds
Tahini	↔	Any Nut Butter
White Wine	↔	Chicken or Veg Stock (with a Splash of White Wine Vinegar)
Worcestershire Sauce	↔	Soy Sauce or Chopped Anchovies
Za'atar	↔	Combo of ½ Sumac, ½ Sesame Seeds

SOMETHING FRESH

TIME
15 MINUTES

SERVES
4 AS A SIDE OR 2 AS A MAIN

VEGGIE

FRESH

BEETROOT & FETA CHAAT

Chaat is one of the most underrated foods in India. It's an all-encompassing salad, fresh, sour, spicy and crunchy. My mum would make this with yoghurt, potatoes and chickpeas, but in my version I've used the sweetness of cooked beetroot with salty feta to achieve a parallel version. Perfect with any curry or just on its own. Traditionally the crunch element would come from papri, which is fried dough, but I've used Bombay mix because it's a bit easier to find. However, if you find any crunchy fried puri in the Indian supermarket, give them a go!

250g cooked beetroot

2 large tomatoes, core removed

1 x 400g tin of chickpeas

½ a red onion

2 green finger chillies

a small handful of fresh mint

3 tbsp tamarind paste

2 tbsp honey   ↔ brown sugar or agave

½ tsp ground cumin

200g Greek yoghurt

100g feta

100g Bombay mix

a small handful of   ⁓ optional
pomegranate seeds

salt

Cut the beetroot into large chunks and the tomatoes into small pieces.

Drain and rinse the chickpeas.

Finely chop the red onion, chillies and mint.

Make the tamarind dressing by combining the tamarind paste with the honey, 2 tablespoons of water and a pinch of ground cumin.

In a bowl, combine the beetroot, tomatoes, chickpeas and onions, lightly season with salt. Spread the yoghurt on your serving plate and top with the beetroot mix.

Drizzle over the tamarind dressing and crumble over the feta, then sprinkle over the chopped mint and chillies and the Bombay mix.

Finish with the pomegranate seeds and a sprinkling of ground cumin, and enjoy.

COOK YOUR OWN BEETROOT
I love pre-cooked beetroot – all the fun without the mess. But if you want to use fresh, roast it at 200°C, brushed with a little oil and wrapped in foil, for 45–60 minutes until tender. Allow to cool before using.

NOTES
→   *You could even drizzle over some green chutney (page 165)*

27

FRESH

BOMBAY FISH FINGER SANDWICH

Bird's Eye fish finger sandwiches are a cherished classic among British after-school snacks, to which Bombay mix adds the perfect crunchy coating without the hassle of deep-frying. This sandwich embodies the fusion of British convenience culture with the spice and crunch of Indian flavours. Nestled between slices of classic white bread – no sourdough here – and slathered with a curried tartare sauce, it's a fantastic choice for a fresh and satisfying lunch

FOR THE BOMBAY FISH

100g Bombay mix

200g white fish (cod is the classic choice)

2 tbsp plain flour

1 egg

FOR THE CURRIED TARTARE SAUCE

1 tbsp gherkins, finely chopped, plus extra, sliced, for the sandwich ↔ 1 large pickle or 6 cornichons

1 tbsp capers, finely chopped

1 green chilli, finely chopped

2 tbsp fresh coriander, chopped

1 clove of garlic

100g mayonnaise

1 tbsp lemon juice

1 tbsp curry powder

salt and pepper

FOR ASSEMBLY

4 thick slices of white bread

4 leaves of butter lettuce

4 tbsp mango chutney ↔ any other chutney

Preheat the oven to 180°C.

Use a food processor to pulse the Bombay mix into large crumbs – you don't want a fine crumb.

Cut the fish into finger-length pieces.

Set up three bowls for a coating station: one with flour, one with a whisked egg, and one with the processed Bombay mix. Season the flour and egg bowls lightly with salt.

Coat each piece of fish in this order: flour, egg and Bombay mix. Make sure to press the coating well on to the fish. Place the coated fish on a baking sheet and bake for 8–10 minutes, or until just cooked through.

While the fish is baking, combine the chopped gherkins, capers, green chilli and coriander in a bowl and grate in the garlic. Add the mayo, lemon juice and curry powder, mix well, and season with salt and pepper.

Once the fish is done, assemble the sandwiches. Spread the curried tartare sauce on two slices of bread. To the other two slices, add the lettuce, fish, chutney and extra sliced gherkins. Sandwich it all together, and enjoy.

ALL I WANT IS SOMETHING ...

NOTES

→ If you're looking for a shortcut, use store-bought tartare sauce.

→ You can freeze the coated fingers uncooked, just like good old Bird's Eye fish fingers.

→ Experiment with various types of Bombay mix, such as Gujarati mix, chakri mix, or even balti mix.

AIR FRYER FRIENDLY

→ Pop the fish fingers into the air fryer using the same time and temperature.

ICY MISO NOODLE SOUP

This is for when it's scorching hot out or when you crave that fresh feeling in your lunch. Icy noodle soups are huge in Korea – I love them, and so should you. They are bright and pungent, and I've used cucumber water for another level of much-needed freshness – bonus points for getting in more liquid when it's so hot outside! This also takes inspiration from a cold Japanese soup called hiyajiru, which uses miso as the base. It's the same comforting feeling of having a hot soup on a cold winter day, but in reverse!

½ a cucumber

2 eggs

200g soba noodles

2 tsp tahini ↔ any nut butter

300ml water

2 tbsp miso paste

1 tsp grated ginger

1 tsp chilli oil

2 tbsp apple cider vinegar ↔ sherry vinegar or white wine vinegar

a pinch of sugar

1 clove of garlic

4 spring onions

300g crushed ice

salt

Smash the cucumber and roughly chop into small pieces. Place in a colander over a bowl, salt with half a teaspoon of sea salt and allow to sit for 15 minutes to draw out the water.

Boil a big pan of water and boil your eggs for 6 minutes, cooking the soba noodles in the same water according to the packet instructions.

Rinse the noodles in cold water and leave until ready to serve.

Peel the eggs and cut in half.

Whisk the tahini to a smooth paste with 4 tablespoons of water. Add the miso and whisk until smooth. Slowly add the remaining water and the ginger.

Squeeze out the water from the cucumbers and add it to the miso broth. Taste for seasoning – depending on how salty your miso is, you may not need any more.

Combine the cucumbers in a bowl with the chilli oil, apple cider vinegar and the pinch of sugar, and grate in the garlic.

Finely slice the spring onions lengthways and soak them in ice water to get them really crisp.

To serve, pile your soba noodles in the centre of a bowl. Fill the outside with crushed ice. Top with the cucumber and egg, and pour the broth over the ice.

Finish with more chilli oil and spring onions, and enjoy.

NOTE

→ *Toast the miso by putting it on a baking tray then grilling on the highest setting for 5 minutes. If you have a gas hob you can spread it over a metal spoon and gently brush it over the flame. It gives another layer of flavour to the miso paste!*

ZINGY CRISPY EGG CABBAGE SALAD

This salad is a burst of flavours and textures: crunchy cabbage, crispy eggs and lots of veg. Salads are great for a quick lunch, and this one is inspired by a spicy zingy som tam, an incredibly spicy and sour papaya salad from Thailand, which I've drizzled with creamy peanut butter. Topped with an ultra-crispy fried egg, you can eat it in the middle of the day for lunch or as a salad with a bigger meal later.

1 small cabbage, thinly sliced, approx. 600g. I used a mixture of white and red

2 carrots, thinly sliced or grated

200g cherry tomatoes, halved

4 tbsp peanut butter ↔ any nut butter

2 eggs

2 tbsp peanuts, toasted and crushed

a small handful of fresh coriander, roughly chopped

salt

FOR THE DRESSING

2 cloves of garlic

3 Thai red chillies ↔ 3 long red chillies

6 tbsp fresh lime juice

4 tbsp fish sauce ↔ veggie fish sauce

2 tbsp light brown sugar

Smash the garlic and chillies with the back of a knife to form a paste – you don't want pieces of the chilli in your sauce. Alternatively, you can blend the two together with the rest of the dressing ingredients.

In a bowl, combine the garlic, chillies, lime juice, fish sauce and brown sugar.

Put all the veg into a large bowl and dress with the spicy dressing, reserving 1 teaspoon of the dressing.

Mix the peanut butter with 4 tablespoons of warm water and the tablespoon of reserved dressing to make a sauce and add a pinch of salt.

Fry the eggs until very crispy.

Plate up the cabbage salads. Drizzle with the peanut sauce, and sprinkle with the crushed peanuts and chopped coriander. Add the fried eggs on top.

NOTE
→ To get the cabbage really thin, use a mandoline, otherwise a sharp knife and a steady hand works great.

HAINANESE SALMON RICE

Hainanese chicken is one of my staple comfort foods. It's the national dish of Singapore, and don't tell the other countries, but it's my favourite of all the national dishes I've ever made. The chicken is poached in a ginger and spring onion broth, which is then used to make the rice and served with a spring onion oil and chilli oil. So incredibly simple but so delicious. This salmon version hits all the right spots, and you still get that crispy salmon skin that we all know and love.

150g sushi rice   ↔ any short-grain rice

5cm ginger

5 spring onions

225ml chicken stock

2 salmon fillets

50ml vegetable oil

1 tbsp sesame oil

salt

crispy chilli oil, to serve

soy sauce, to serve

Wash the rice three times in cold water until it runs almost clear.

Cut 2 slices of the ginger and leave the rest for later. Cut the whites off the spring onions and roughly chop.

Put the rice into a pan with the chicken stock, sliced ginger, spring onion whites and ½ teaspoon of salt.

Bring the rice to a simmer. Place the salmon on top of the rice, skin side up, turn the heat to low and put a lid on. Allow to simmer for 10 minutes.

Meanwhile, finely chop the remaining spring onions and ginger, and place in a heatproof bowl. Heat the vegetable oil to smoking point and pour over the spring onion and ginger. Add a pinch of salt and set aside.

Heat the sesame oil until very hot. Remove the salmon from the rice, brushing off any rice pieces. Put the lid back on the rice to allow it to steam. Place the salmon skin side down in the hot oil and cook for 1 minute, just to crisp up the skin.

Stir the rice well and taste for seasoning,
Serve the rice with the salmon, and drizzle over the spring onion oil, chilli oil and soy sauce.

QUICK CHILLI OIL

Crispy chilli oil is readily available in most supermarkets but if you want a speedy alternative, heat 50ml of vegetable oil in a pan and add the 3 cloves of garlic, 1 shallot and 4 red chillies, all finely chopped. Cook on a medium heat for 6–7 minutes, until the oil is stained red. Transfer to a bowl and mix in ¼ teaspoon of salt and 1 tbsp soy sauce.

NOTES

→   *Use any fish you like! You can also use chicken, but just make sure it's boneless so it cooks in the same time as the rice. My favourite is to use bone-in chicken thighs with the skin on, removing the bone and crisping up the skin just like the salmon at the end.*

→   *You can use shop-bought crispy chilli oil and skip the quick one I've made here – that way you'll save 15 minutes and have it done in half an hour.*

ALL I WANT IS SOMETHING…

FRESH

CRISPY GINGER & LIME BEAN SALAD

I've been trying to get into beans, and this bean salad has become my holy grail for meal prep lunches. Baking the beans makes them crispy and perfect for soaking up the sour lime dressing, all served on a big pile of whipped cottage cheese for some added protein and bursts of sweetness from the pomegranate. So if you aren't sure about beans yet, this may just be the one to convert you!

1 x 400g tin of chickpeas	
1 x 400g tin of butter beans	
1 x 400g tin of red kidney beans	
½ tsp ground cumin	
1 tbsp plain flour	
2 tbsp nutritional yeast	↔ Parmesan or any hard cheese
2 sticks of celery, finely sliced	
150g sugar snap peas, chopped in half lengthways	
olive oil	

FOR THE DRESSING

5cm ginger, grated	
3 limes	
50ml extra virgin olive oil	
1 tsp miso paste	↔ 2 tbsp soy sauce and 1 tsp tahini
1 tsp honey	
½ tsp salt	
½ tsp black pepper	

TO SERVE

250g cottage cheese	↔ ricotta or thick yoghurt
a large handful of fresh parsley, finely chopped	
½ tsp salt	

Preheat the oven to 180°C.

Drain the chickpeas and the beans and lightly rinse them. Put them into a bowl and toss with the cumin powder, plain flour and nutritional yeast (if using).

Place in a single layer on a baking sheet and drizzle with olive oil. Bake for 25–30 minutes, until the beans are crispy, tossing them halfway through. Allow to cool fully, then put them into a bowl.

Meanwhile, combine all the ingredients for the dressing.

Blend the cottage cheese, parsley and salt.

Add the sugar snaps and celery to the bowl of beans and toss with the dressing. Taste for seasoning.

Spread the cottage cheese on a plate and pile the crispy beans on top.

NOTE

→   *This is a great way to use up any leftover beans you have in the back of the cupboard – just throw in what you have!*

41

FRESH

TOMATO CAESAR-ESQUE SALAD

Anything to do with Caesar salad is always fantastic. When tomatoes are bursting into season, this salty savoury dressing is perfect with them. I opted for no mayo in this dressing, to keep it crisp and refreshing – think of it like panzanella meets Caesar salad! The tomatoes will soak up that savoury dressing, and add a burst of seasonal sweetness. And don't forget the whole anchovies on top for that delicious savoury saltiness.

150g crusty stale bread	
100g thick-cut bacon or lardons, cut into thick pieces	⌁ optional
4 anchovies in oil, plus more to serve	
juice of 1 lemon	
1 tsp Dijon mustard	
1 tbsp Worcestershire sauce	↔ soy sauce
2 tbsp red wine vinegar	↔ apple cider or white wine vinegar
2 cloves of garlic, grated	
50g Parmesan, plus more to serve	
50ml extra virgin olive oil	
500g tomatoes	
1 large handful of fresh basil	
salt	

Preheat the oven to 180°C.

Tear the bread into large chunks, a similar size to the tomatoes. Add to a tray with the bacon and drizzle over the oil from the anchovy jar, and bake in the oven for 15 minutes, until golden and crisp.

Finely chop the anchovies, mushing them with the knife to form a paste. Put them into a bowl and whisk in the juice of the lemon, the Dijon mustard, Worcestershire sauce and red wine vinegar. Add the grated garlic and the Parmesan. Finally, whisk in the olive oil.

Chop the tomatoes into large chunks and toss them in a bowl with a large pinch of salt. Leave them to sit for 5 minutes, then add the dressing. Once the croutons have cooled, add them to the bowl and mix together very well so that the bread can absorb the dressing.

Throw in the fresh basil leaves last of all, top with additional whole anchovies, add a sprinkling of Parmesan and enjoy immediately.

NOTES

→   Skip the whole anchovies if you aren't a fan. But keep the ones in the dressing and mash them up well – they add such a great savouriness that can't be missed!

→   Using seasonal tomatoes is what is really going to make them shine, especially if you can find the beautiful heritage ones! If you are going to splurge on anything for this dish, make it the tomatoes. Tomato season in the UK is from June to September.

AIR FRYER FRIENDLY

→   Crisp up the croutons and bacon in the air fryer using the same time and temperature you would the oven, checking after 5 minutes and shaking regularly.

ALL I WANT IS SOMETHING …

LOADED SUMMER ROLLS

Vietnamese summer rolls are always my go-to fresh food when I feel like I need lots of delicious vegetables all wrapped up in a little bundle. They are great to take with you on the go, and fantastic for using up bits in the fridge. I've combined these summer rolls with an equally as delicious Malaysian roll called popiah. Popiah have sauce slathered on the inside and are packed to the brim with crunchy onions and nuts, which is exactly what I want in my summer rolls.

200g vermicelli rice noodles

200g portobello mushrooms, cut into 1cm slices

¼ tsp sugar

1 clove of garlic, grated

100g beansprouts

5 eggs

8 rice paper rounds

5 tbsp hoisin

5 tbsp sriracha

a small handful of fresh coriander, roughly chopped

1 baby gem lettuce, shredded

1 cucumber, cut into thin batons

4 tbsp roasted salted peanuts, roughly chopped

3 tbsp crispy shallots

vegetable oil

salt

FOR THE FISH SAUCE DIPPING SAUCE

50ml fish sauce   ↔ veggie fish sauce

2 cloves of garlic, finely chopped

1 red chilli, finely chopped

3 tbsp hot water

1 tbsp sugar

juice of 1 lime

Place the vermicelli noodles in a heatproof bowl. Pour boiling water over them and allow them to soak for 3–4 minutes (check the packet instructions), then drain and rinse in cold water.

Put the mushrooms into a dry non-stick frying pan with a big pinch of salt and cook for 5 minutes on a high heat, to draw out the moisture from the mushrooms. Once the mushrooms are browned, add 1 tablespoon of oil, the sugar and the garlic. Cook for 2 minutes, until the mushrooms are crisp, then remove from the pan and set aside.

Heat the pan with a small glug of oil and fry off the beansprouts for 30 seconds with a pinch of salt, until just softened.

Whisk the eggs in a bowl and add to the same non-stick pan (no need to wash it). Cook on each side for 2 minutes, to make a thin plain omelette. Roll up the omelette and cut it into 1cm slices.

Pour some cold water on to a plate, checking it fits your rice paper rounds. Soak one of the rounds for no more than 30 seconds, making sure all of it touches the water. Place it on your chopping board – don't worry if it's not totally soft yet, as it will soften as you add the fillings.

Brush over 1 teaspoon each of hoisin and sriracha. Then add the mushrooms, omelette strips, coriander, lettuce, beansprouts, rice noodles, cucumber, peanuts and crispy shallots.

Fold the right and left sides into the middle like a book. Then roll like a burrito to make your summer roll. Repeat with the rest of the rice paper rounds and filling.

For the fish sauce dipping sauce, combine all the ingredients in a small bowl, mixing well so the sugar is dissolved.

Serve the summer rolls with the dipping sauce.

PEANUT DIPPING SAUCE

If you are vegetarian or would just prefer a peanut dipping sauce, whisk together 3 tablespoons of peanut butter with 1 tablespoon of hoisin, 1 tablespoon of soy sauce, 1 tablespoon of sriracha and 3 tablespoons of hot water.

ALL I WANT IS SOMETHING …

TIME
20 MINUTES

SERVES
2

VEGGIE

AIR FRYER

FRESH

PEACH & HALLOUMI TACOS

The sweet honeyed flavour of peaches and the salty crispy halloumi make these tacos brim with fresh flavours in no time. I've led with peaches here as they are more accessible, but when you can get hold of perfectly ripe figs – and unfortunately this is only for a precious two weeks a year – you need to make sure to stock up and indulge as much as you can.

If you can get your hands on some hot honey, that would be perfect here!

5 peaches, quartered ↔ 4 figs

½ a red onion, finely chopped

2 green chillies, finely chopped

1 tbsp olive oil

3 tbsp sour cream ↔ yoghurt

1 spring onion

a small handful of fresh coriander, finely chopped

juice of 1 lime

250g halloumi

8–10 corn tortillas

½ tsp chilli flakes

4 tbsp honey

salt and black pepper

hot sauce (I like El Yucateco or Cholula), to serve

Combine the peaches, red onion and 1 green chilli in a bowl, season with salt, pepper and 1 tablespoon of olive oil.

Blitz up the sour cream, the remaining green chilli, spring onion, coriander and lime. Season with salt and pepper.

Chop up the halloumi into small pieces and cook in a hot pan with a drizzle of oil until golden and crispy.

Combine the chilli flakes and honey in a microwave-safe jar and warm for 30 seconds to 1 minute in the microwave, until bubbling.

Heat up the tortillas and layer the green sauce with the peaches and halloumi. Finally drizzle with the honey and hot sauce, if you like, and enjoy.

HOT HONEY
If you love hot honey, empty a jar of honey into a saucepan with a few teaspoons of chilli flakes and heat until bubbling. Leave to cool then decant back into the honey jar and use as normal.

AIR FRYER FRIENDLY
→ *If you prefer, cook the halloumi in the air fryer for a few minutes until crisp and golden .*

ALL I WANT IS SOMETHING …

SPICY & SOUR GREEN BEANS WITH TUNA

This recipe came about when I'd come back from a long weekend away, eating out and drinking, and just needed something nourishing but still special. It ended up being a mix of a tuna niçoise and a som tam. It's very sour and spicy, which ties all the veg together perfectly and makes you feel so good after.

300g baby potatoes, halved

2 eggs

50g green beans, trimmed

1 baby gem lettuce, leaves torn

1 shallot, thinly sliced

½ a cucumber, sliced

100g cherry tomatoes, halved

1 tin of tuna, drained

FOR THE DRESSING

2–3 Thai red chillies, finely chopped/pounded   ↔ 2 tsp spicy chilli oil

3 tbsp fish sauce

juice of 2 limes

1 tsp sugar

2 cloves of garlic, grated

salt

TO SERVE

a small handful of peanuts, crushed

fresh coriander

chilli oil

Bring a large pot of salted water to the boil, then add the potatoes and boil for 15 minutes. In the final 6 minutes add the eggs, and in the final 4 minutes add the green beans. Drain.

Peel the eggs and cut in half.

Combine the ingredients for the dressing and season with salt.

Toss the potatoes, green beans, baby gem, shallots, cucumber and cherry tomatoes in a bowl with most of the dressing.

Transfer to a serving bowl and top with the tuna, eggs and the remaining dressing.

Sprinkle with the peanuts, coriander and extra chilli oil, if needed.

NOTE

→   For milder heat, use long red chillies. If you can pound the Thai red chillies and garlic in a pestle and mortar, you won't get big pieces of chilli in your salad! You can also soak the sliced shallots in ice water so they are not as pungent.

ALL I WANT IS ...

SOMETHING SALTY & SAVOURY

GLASS-SHATTERINGLY CRISPY KIMCHI & POTATO PANCAKES

Korean kimchi pancakes are to die for, but I wanted them glass-crackingly crispy. I make these in a similar way to latkes, the fantastically crisp Jewish potato fritters, which makes them incredibly crispy, sour and a little spicy. And the Parmesan crust just makes them even more delicious and more crunchy.

300g white potatoes, peeled and grated

150g kimchi, finely chopped

2 tbsp plain flour

1 tbsp cornflour

1 egg

1 tbsp gochujang

½ tsp sugar

½ tsp salt

50g Parmesan cheese, grated ↔ Veggie Parmesan or any hard cheese

150g crème fraîche ↔ sour cream

1 tbsp sesame oil

1 tbsp honey

vegetable oil

Combine the potatoes and kimchi and squeeze out as much liquid as possible with your hands or inside a clean tea towel.

Put the squeezed veg into a bowl and add the plain flour, cornflour, egg, gochujang, sugar and salt. Mix well.

Heat 1cm of vegetable oil in a non-stick frying pan and when it's hot, add a few tablespoons of the batter, flattening them out into thin circles. Fry for 3 minutes on each side, then place on a wire rack to drain.

Pile the parmesan directly on to the non-stick frying pan in heaps a similar size to the pancakes. Add the pancake on top and allow the Parmesan to crisp up. Place back on the wire rack to cool and crisp up further.

In a bowl, combine the crème fraîche, sesame oil, honey and a pinch of salt.

Serve the crispy fritters with a dollop of the crème fraîche, and enjoy.

NOTES

→ When buying kimchi, ingredients such as fish sauce or shrimp paste guarantee an umami boost, but look for versions without if you're veggie! And try looking for jars with a close expiry date, meaning they have been fermenting longer and will be more zingy! A good kimchi is zingy, crunchy and a little spicy.

→ If you aren't a fan of kimchi, try sauerkraut.

→ Starchy potatoes such as russets are best for these, but in a pinch any white potato will work!

55

ALL I WANT IS SOMETHING…

SALTY & SAVOURY

GARLICKY ANCHOVY BUTTER SMASHED POTATOES

Anchovies are a new love affair of mine, and now I can't get enough of them. They bring the perfect blend of saltiness and brininess, and a punch of flavour to any dish. Here I've taken the little fishes, mashed them up with some butter, and generously spread this umami goodness all over crispy potatoes. All balanced by the dreamy sour cream dip – perfect for that salty craving.

500g baby potatoes

75g butter

4 cloves of garlic, grated

10 anchovies, finely chopped

50ml vegetable oil

FOR THE SOUR CREAM DIP

a large handful of fresh chives	↔ spring onions, finely chopped

1 tbsp onion powder

juice of ½ a lemon

250g sour cream

salt and black pepper

Put the potatoes into a pot of lightly salted cold water. Bring to the boil, then reduce the heat to a simmer and cook for about 15 minutes, or until the potatoes are fork-tender.

Meanwhile, preheat your oven to 230°C.

In a saucepan, melt the butter and add the garlic and anchovies. Cook this mixture for about 5 minutes, or until the butter starts to brown, then turn off the heat.

Set aside 1 tablespoon of chives for garnish, then put the rest into a bowl and combine with the onion powder, lemon juice, sour cream and freshly ground black pepper. Season with salt.

Once the potatoes are cooked, drain them and transfer them to a baking tray. Using the back of a cup or something similar, gently smash each potato, being careful to keep them mostly intact.

Drizzle the smashed potatoes generously with oil, lightly sprinkle them with salt, and roast them in the oven for 20–25 minutes, turning them halfway through. Once the potatoes are nice and crispy, brush them generously with the anchovy butter.

To serve, spread the sour cream dip on a plate, place the crispy potatoes on top, and finish with more anchovy butter and a sprinkling of the reserved chives.

NOTES

→ If you're on a trip to Italy or Portugal, stockpile anchovies and bring them back in your hand luggage, if under 100ml.

→ If you're not quite sold on anchovies (though I urge you to give them a try because they're delightful), you can try swapping them for a tablespoon of miso, a teaspoon of Marmite, a handful of Parmesan, or a few chopped rashers of cooked bacon!

AIR FRYER FRIENDLY

→ Bake the potatoes in the air fryer using the same time and temperature you would the oven.

CHEESE & ONION BOREK

Cheese and onion pasties are iconic. They are the perfect train snack, and it was my go-to Greggs pasty flavour whenever we ventured out of my hometown of Slough and into the depths of London. I've used this filling inside Turkish börek, a incredibly crispy filo-wrapped pasty – so you get the gooey cheese and onion flavour we all know and love, inside a glass-shatteringly crispy shell.

3 large onions, roughly chopped

125g butter

3 cloves of garlic, chopped

500g potatoes, peeled and cut into chunks

200g strong Cheddar, grated   ↔ your favourite cheese

1 tsp fresh thyme

½ tsp black pepper

½ tsp salt

100ml double cream

250g filo pastry (8 sheets)

1 tsp nigella seeds   ↔ sesame seeds
⌁ optional

Preheat the oven to 180°C and line a baking sheet with baking paper.

Put the onions into a large pot with 25g of the butter and a pinch of salt. Cook on a medium heat for 20–25 minutes, until golden and caramelized. Add the garlic and cook for a further 3 minutes.

Meanwhile, put your potatoes into a large pan of water and bring to the boil. Boil for 15 minutes, or until fork tender, then drain.

Set aside one handful of grated cheese to top the pies before they bake.

Put the potatoes into a large bowl. Add the caramelized onions, thyme, black pepper, salt, double cream and the grated cheese. Mash together and taste for seasoning.

Melt the remaining 100g of butter in a small pan. Lay one sheet of filo on the work surface and brush liberally with the melted butter. Add another layer of filo and brush again.

Spoon a quarter of the potato mixture along the longest edge and roll up the filo, encasing the potato filling to make a tube. Then roll again to make a snail shape, pressing it in tightly. Place on your baking tray, brush with some more butter, and sprinkle with the reserved cheese and some nigella seeds.

Repeat with the remaining filo and filling.

Bake in the oven for 20 minutes, or until very crispy.

Allow to cool slightly, or serve at room temperature.

AIR FRYER FRIENDLY

→   Bake the borek in the air fryer using the same time and temperature.

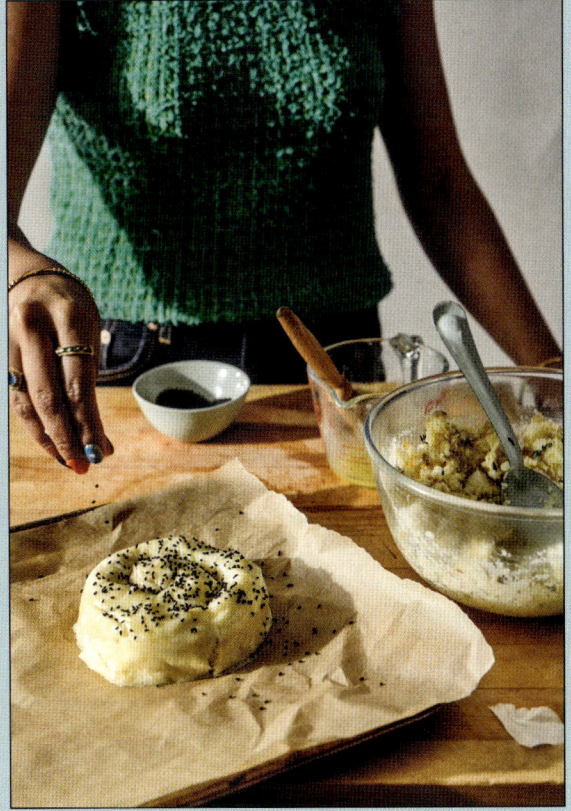

SECRET CHEESY MASALA EGG MUFFIN

Eggs in Gujarat are a fantastic night-time food staple – take note of the importance of night-time. Because Gujarat is largely vegetarian and eggs are classed as meat, many women don't approve of their husbands eating them, so they sneak out at night to go in secret to satisfy their cravings, and boy, they are delicious. I think the secrecy makes them that much more spectacular. You get almost every variety of egg, smothered in spices. My favourite was the masala scrambled egg, which I've placed inside a traditional English muffin, with crunchy bacon and quick curried ketchup.

½ a red onion, finely chopped

1 green chilli (finger chilli), finely chopped

¼ of a bell pepper, finely chopped

1 clove of garlic, grated

½ tsp grated ginger

½ tsp chilli powder

½ tsp garam masala

4 rashers smoked bacon   ⌁ optional

2 English muffins

4 eggs

50g Cheddar cheese

5 cherry tomatoes, quartered

1 tbsp butter

2 slices of American cheese

3 tbsp tomato ketchup

½ tsp garam masala   ↔ curry powder

salt and black pepper

In a non-stick pan, gently fry the red onion, green chilli, bell pepper, garlic, ginger, chilli powder and garam masala for 5 minutes on a low heat, until the spices are bubbling and the vegetables have softened.

Remove from the heat and transfer to a bowl. Allow the pan to totally cool down.

If using, fry the bacon to your liking in another frying pan (or in the oven), then heat up the muffins in the bacon grease or warm in a toaster.

Crack the eggs into the bowl of vegetables, then grate in the Cheddar and add the tomatoes. Gently mix together so that the spices are evenly distributed, and add ¼ teaspoon of salt.

Add the butter to the now cooled non-stick pan, and pour in the egg mixture. Turn the heat to the lowest setting and cook the eggs, using a spatula and folding to create very soft scrambled eggs.

Portion into two rounds in the pan and add a slice of American cheese to the top of each one. Pop a lid on top for 30 seconds and allow the cheese to melt.

Mix together the ketchup and garam masala. Add a tablespoon of spicy ketchup to the bottom half of each muffin, then add a portion of cheesy eggs, some slices of bacon and close with the top of the muffin.

NOTE
→   *Try the eggs in between two soft pieces of white bread, for a spicy egg sando.*

ALL I WANT IS SOMETHING ...

SALTY & SAVOUR

SMOKY, STICKY SOY-BRAISED TOFU

Smoked tofu is like discovering a hidden gem in the supermarket. It infuses a delightful smokiness throughout a dish, creating an incredible depth of flavour. I've concocted a spicy-sweet sauce to drench the tofu, and it all comes together in under 30 minutes. (And guess what? It's air fryer friendly!)

250g block of firm smoked tofu, sliced into thin squares

5 cloves of garlic

4cm ginger

1 tsp five-spice powder

3 tbsp hoisin ↔ honey

4 tbsp soy sauce

1 tbsp Shaoxing rice wine ↔ dry sherry, white wine or mirin

½ tsp chilli flakes

2 star anise

4 cloves

1 cinnamon stick

1 onion, cut into large chunks

vegetable oil

Pan-fry the tofu slices in a little oil for 2 minutes on each side, until they turn golden.

Grate the garlic and ginger into a jug and add the five-spice powder, hoisin, soy sauce, Shaoxing rice wine, chilli flakes and the whole spices.

Heat a wok on a high heat, add a little oil, then add the onions and fry for about 3 minutes, until they soften. Add the sauce mixture along with 150ml of water, and bring to the boil. Add the tofu and cook for 5 minutes, until the sauce thickens and coats the tofu.

Serve the tofu over a bowl of hot rice and enjoy!

NOTES

→   If you haven't got whole spices, don't fret – use ¼ teaspoon of ground, or simply omit them.

→   And if you can't find smoked tofu, regular firm tofu will work, but you'll miss out on that delectable smoky flavour.

AIR FRYER FRIENDLY

→   For an equally delicious result, pop the tofu into the air fryer at 200°C for 10–15 minutes, until it turns golden.

65

ALL I WANT IS SOMETHING...

PRAWN & SPRING ONION PAKORA

An iconic British Chinese takeaway staple, prawn toast, combined with my favourite Indian snack, bhajia (or pakora as you might call them). The fried bread makes these extra crispy, with pockets of juicy prawns for all the things you love in a prawn toast. My tip is to add spinach for some crunch and a few tablespoons of Parmesan for an extra savouriness – don't worry, it won't taste cheesy! Dunk these in some sweet chilli sauce for a banging snack.

300g shelled raw prawns

100g crusty stale white bread

1 bunch of spring onions, roughly chopped

2 cloves of garlic, minced

1 tsp minced ginger

4 tbsp sesame seeds + extra for sprinkling

2 tbsp Parmesan, grated

1 tsp light soy sauce

¼ tsp white pepper

½ tsp salt

75g plain flour

1 tsp baking powder

a large handful of baby spinach

vegetable oil, for deep-frying

sweet chilli sauce, to serve

Keeping aside 100g of the prawns with their tails on, roughly chop the rest of them, with a mix of small and big pieces for texture. Tear the bread into chunks similar to the prawns.

Put the prawns, spring onions, garlic, ginger, sesame seeds, Parmesan, soy sauce, white pepper and salt into a bowl. Mix well, then add the flour, bread, baking powder, 75ml of water and baby spinach. Mix with your hands.

Heat up enough oil for deep-frying to around 175°C. Gently, using your hands (this creates the best crunchy texture, rather than spoons), form 3 tbsp of batter into a round in your hand, top with a tail-on prawn and sprinkle with sesame seeds.

Fry for 5–6 minutes, until golden brown and crispy. Drain on a paper towel and enjoy with sweet chilli sauce.

SALTY & SAVOURY

ALL I WANT IS SOMETHING …

CARAMELIZED HONEY & ZA'ATAR CHEESE TOASTIE

SALTY & SAVOUR

I love the combination of salty and sweet – honey and cheese are my go-to fridge snacks when I need a quick bite. Toasting the outside of the bread with caramelized honey gives a slightly nutty but very chewy texture that makes these toasties to die for.

25g mature Cheddar cheese	
25g Gruyère cheese	↔ Comte or more Cheddar
2 tbsp butter	
2 slices of sourdough bread	↔ crusty white bread
2 tbsp honey	
1 tbsp za'atar + more for sprinkling	
sea salt flakes	
pickled chillies, to serve	

Grate both cheeses and combine in a bowl.

Spread the butter liberally on both sides of the bread and stuff the grated cheese and za'atar between them, reserving about 1 tablespoon of cheese.

Put a frying pan on a low heat and add the toastie. Cook very gently for 10 minutes, until the cheese is bubbling and hot, and the outside is golden and crisp. Add a splash of water and put the lid on to help the cheese melt.

Sprinkle half the reserved cheese directly on to the pan and put the toastie on top – the cheese will melt and caramelize on to the bread. Repeat on the other side.

Take the toastie out of the pan and turn the heat off. Drizzle the honey and za'atar into the hot pan and allow them to bubble. Put the toastie back into the pan and swirl it around in the honey.

Remove from the pan and sprinkle with more za'atar and flaky sea salt.

Cut the toastie into pieces and enjoy hot, with a pickle.

NOTE

→ Use whatever combination of cheeses you like. And play about with different spice mixes such as 1 tsp ras el hanout or even Old Bay seasoning if you don't have any za'atar.

ALL I WANT IS SOMETHING …

CHEAT'S LEEK & BRIE SPANISH TORTILLA

If you've been reading through this book you'll know I love a good hack, or anything to save me some time or faff in the kitchen. I always seem to have frozen oven chips in the freezer, and this makes perfect use of them, coating them with caramelized leeks and Brie cheese to make a gooey Spanish tortilla.

600g frozen thick-cut oven chips (skinless)

50ml extra virgin olive oil

1 large leek, thinly sliced

6 cloves of garlic, thinly sliced

6 eggs

200g Brie cheese

salt

Preheat the oven to 200°C. Place the oven chips on an oven tray, liberally cover with half the olive oil and bake for 15 minutes.

Add the leeks and garlic to a pan with 2 tbsp of oil. Cook these down for 20 minutes with a big pinch of salt until very soft and caramelized.

Put all the eggs into a large bowl and very gently mix together – you don't want them completely combined. Add the leeks, garlic, and chips and allow to sit for 10 minutes.

Meanwhile, cut the cheese into thick slices.

Pour a small glug of oil into a 22cm non-stick pan and pour in half the chip and leek batter.

Layer on the thick slices of Brie and top with the rest of the batter.

Put a lid on the pan and cook on a low-medium heat for 15 minutes, until the cheese is very melty, but the top of the eggs is still soft.

Flip over on to a plate and slide the tortilla back into the pan. Cook for 30 seconds more and then flip on to a plate and enjoy while hot.

NOTES

→ Switch out the Brie with any gooey cheese you like, maybe Taleggio, fontina or even reblochon if you're feeling fancy.

→ You can also use this as a base for any flavour of Spanish tortilla – add some chorizo, some caramelized onions . . . you would be surprised how many things go well with potatoes and eggs.

CHORIZO & PEA POZOLE

One of my favourite soups in Mexico was pozole. The base is surprisingly light, but it's topped with lots of hearty vegetables and crunchy bits, making it full of textures and flavours, so every bite is different from the last. Traditionally it's made with hominy, which is produced from dried corn, but I've used peas in mine, roasted to get that nutty sweet flavour. The chorizo gives an extra depth of flavour, similar to Mexican dried chillies!

600g frozen peas

500g chorizo   ↔ spicy sausage

1 tsp cumin seeds

1 tbsp chipotle paste

1 tomato, roughly chopped

½ an onion, roughly chopped

6 cloves of garlic, roughly chopped

2 litres chicken stock

olive oil

salt and black pepper

FOR THE TOPPINGS

¼ of a white cabbage, shredded

5 radishes, diced   ↔ celery

a small handful of fresh coriander, finely chopped

100g tortilla chips

1 tsp dried oregano

2 limes

Preheat the oven to 200°C.

Pour half your peas on to a baking tray, drizzle with oil and sprinkle with salt. Roast for 20 minutes, or until very crispy, stirring halfway through.

Slice half the chorizo and crumble the rest with your hands. Put this into a dry pan with the cumin seeds and cook for 10 minutes, to render the fat.

Meanwhile, blitz the chipotle paste, tomato, onion and garlic with 200ml of chicken stock in a food processor, until smooth.

Add the blended tomato mix and remaining chicken stock to the pan with 1 teaspoon of salt and bring to a simmer. Allow to cook for 15 minutes.

Add the uncooked peas to the pan and cook for 2 minutes.

Divide the soup between bowls, and top with the crunchy peas, shredded cabbage, radishes, coriander and a handful of tortilla chips. Sprinkle with oregano, squeeze the juice of half a lime into each bowl, and enjoy.

ALL I WANT IS SOMETHING …

SALTY & SAVOUR

CRISPY RICE & 'SEAWEED' SALAD

One of my all-time favourite dishes was at Chet's in London, where I first tried the wonders of the very spicy crispy rice salad, also known as nam khao tod. It's a fantastic combination of crispy rice pockets and fresh herbs, and a classic Chinese takeaway hack of making kale taste like seaweed! I've been using it as my go-to method for using up leftover rice, and I love it so much that I sometimes make extra rice just to have leftovers for this salad.

200g curly kale, stems removed, leaves torn into small pieces

1½ tsp sugar, plus 2 tbsp for the dressing

1 tsp MSG

6 cloves of garlic

4–6 Thai red chillies

5cm ginger, roughly chopped

approx. 500g cooked rice

2 tbsp cornflour

1 shallot, thinly sliced

3 tbsp fish sauce   ↔ veggie fish sauce

3 tbsp lime juice

a small handful each of fresh mint + coriander, chopped

1 stick of celery, sliced

a small handful of peanuts, toasted and chopped

2 baby gem lettuces

vegetable oil

salt

NOTES

→   *If you don't have any day-old rice, you can cook 250g of rice as usual. Spread the hot rice on a tray and leave it to cool down, then dust it with cornflour and you're ready to continue with the recipe.*

→   *You can also make the rice crispy in the oven or air fryer. Just drizzle a tray with oil, spread over the rice, and bake at 200°C for about 30 minutes, giving it a good stir every 10 minutes until very golden and crisp.*

→   *I've left the type of rice unspecified as it truly doesn't matter. I've prepared this salad with various types of rice, and it always turns out fantastic. Just make sure it's a day old, and nice and cold.*

Preheat the oven to 220°C.

Toss the kale with 2 tablespoons of oil, ½ teaspoon of salt, 1 teaspoon of sugar and the MSG. Spread out on a baking tray and roast in the oven for 5 minutes, until very crispy.

Pound the garlic, chillies and ginger together in a pestle and mortar. Add 3 tablespoons of oil, 1 teaspoon of salt and ½ teaspoon of sugar. Mix well. Alternatively, you can blend it all in a hand blender.

Place the mixture in a microwaveable bowl and microwave on high for 2 minutes until it starts sizzling.

Combine the cooked rice with the cornflour. Toss it well with your hands, then add the microwaved oil mixture and mix well.

Heat a cast-iron frying pan over a high heat. Add a generous amount of oil – enough to cover the bottom of the pan. Add the rice in a thin layer and press it down firmly. Reduce the heat to medium and cook for 10 minutes without stirring, until the rice at the bottom of the pan has become very crispy and golden.

Carefully flip the rice disk using a spatula. If it breaks apart, don't worry. Cook on the other side for 5 minutes, until it's golden, then remove it from the pan and let it drain on kitchen paper to remove excess oil. Break it into shards.

While the rice is cooking, soak the shallots in ice-cold water.

Make the dressing by combining the fish sauce, 2 tablespoons of sugar, the lime juice and 3 tablespoons of warm water. Mix well to dissolve the sugar.

Drain the shallots and toss with the rice, herbs, celery and the crispy kale. Dress with the fish sauce dressing and top with the toasted peanuts. Separate the baby gem leaves and use them to scoop up the rice.

ALL I WANT IS SOMETHING …

SOMETHING SPICY

SAMBAL FISH SAUCE WINGS WITH COOLING SPRING ONION DIP

SPICY

Sambal is one of my favourite ingredients to keep on hand, it's a Malaysian-style chilli paste and it can be made in hundreds of different ways, and when you find your perfect version you won't be able to get enough of it. Smother it on chicken wings, with lots of fish sauce to add a zinginess and freshness for the perfect bite. I've even dunked the wings in a cooling garlicky spring onion sauce – in homage to Frank's buffalo wings with a blue cheese sauce!

1kg chicken wings

4 long red chillies

½ tsp chilli flakes

8 cloves of garlic

3cm ginger

1 stick of lemongrass ⸺ optional

3 shallots

1 tbsp tomato purée

4 tbsp sugar

50ml fish sauce

juice of 2 limes

50g butter

vegetable oil

FOR THE GARLIC AND SPRING ONION SAUCE

5 spring onions, finely chopped

5 cloves of garlic, grated

75g mayonnaise

75g sour cream

1 tbsp lime juice

salt and black pepper

Preheat the oven to 220°C.

Pat the wings dry with kitchen paper and liberally salt on both sides. Place them on a baking tray and bake for 20 minutes, then turn and bake for another 10 minutes, until golden and crispy.

Meanwhile, blitz up the chillies, chilli flakes, garlic and ginger in a food processor, adding 2 tablespoons of water to help it blend.

Heat up 50ml vegetable oil in a heavy-bottomed pan. Add the blended chillies and cook for 10 minutes, until the oil is stained red.

Bash the lemongrass with the back of a knife so the fibres come loose, then roughly chop. Blend the shallots and lemongrass together.

Add the blended shallots and lemongrass to the chilli paste, along with the tomato purée, and cook for 10 minutes on a medium heat until thickened and dark red.

Whisk in the sugar, fish sauce, lime juice and butter. Taste for salt – it may not need more, depending on how salty the fish sauce is.

Mix together all the ingredients for the garlic and spring onion sauce and season with ½ teaspoon of salt and black pepper.

Once the wings are cooked, place them in a bowl and pour in the sambal. Toss well so they are evenly coated.

Serve with the garlic and spring onion sauce, and enjoy.

NOTES

→ You can easily double my sambal recipe and keep it in the fridge for up to a month.

→ Use 4 tablespoons of a store-bought sambal for a really quick version!

ALL I WANT IS SOMETHING…

SINGAPORE CHILLI PRAWN BURGERS

One of my favourite things that I ate in Singapore was chilli crab, a cultural icon. A sweet and tomatoey sauce, enriched by eggs and used to smother giant crabs. We also got a black pepper butter crab which was so buttery and peppery. We ended up combining the two crabs and it created the most delicious bite you could have imagined – peppery, spicy and slightly sweet. I've encompassed that glorious bite into a burger.

To make it more budget friendly I've opted for prawns instead of crab, but feel free to switch out the prawns for 250g lump crab meat, or even any cooked fish for an easy fish patty.

FOR THE PRAWN PATTIES

250g raw peeled prawns

2 spring onions, finely chopped

1 egg white

½ tsp white pepper

2 tbsp soy sauce

¼ tsp salt

100g breadcrumbs

FOR THE SAUCE

½ an onion, roughly chopped

4 cloves of garlic, roughly chopped

1cm ginger, grated

3 long red chillies, roughly chopped

½ tsp chilli powder

1 tsp black peppercorns, crushed

4 tbsp tomato ketchup

1 tbsp soy sauce

TO SERVE

4 spring onions, finely sliced

juice of 1 lime

2 burger buns

4 tbsp mayonnaise

1 tsp sesame oil

½ a clove of garlic

butter lettuce

Very finely chop half of the prawns (or blitz them in a food processor) and roughly chop the rest. Put them into a bowl with the spring onions, egg white, white pepper, soy sauce, salt and 50g of the breadcrumbs.

Divide the mixture into two and shape into patties. They'll be a bit sticky, so press them into the remaining breadcrumbs to coat evenly. Place the patties on a plate in the fridge while you make the sauce.

Put the onion, garlic, ginger and chillies into a bowl with a splash of water and use a handheld blender to blitz them to a smooth paste (you can also finely chop them).

Heat a generous glug of oil in a saucepan and sauté the paste for 5 minutes. Add the tomato ketchup, soy sauce and 100ml water. Cook for 2 mins, mix well, and once combined, turn off the heat. Taste and season with salt.

Heat about 4cm of oil in a frying pan and gently shallow-fry the prawn patties for 5 minutes, or until golden on all sides. Once they are cooked, transfer them to a plate lined with kitchen paper to absorb any excess oil, then return the pan to the heat and toast the burger buns until golden.

Combine the 4 spring onions with a pinch of salt and the lime juice.

Combine the mayo and sesame oil and grate in the ½ clove of garlic.

Now to assemble the burger: spread the mayo generously on the bottom half of the bun. Add a few leaves of lettuce, the patty and then the spicy sauce and zesty spring onions. Seal with the top half of the bun and enjoy!

NOTE

→ Don't let any leftover sauce go to waste! It's fantastic for sandwiches or drizzled over some rice with a fried egg.

CRISPY CHILLI CUMIN LAMB

If your Chinese takeaway order is the classic crispy shredded beef, you are going to love his spicier, punchier girlfriend – crispy, juicy lamb in a sticky coating of chilli and cumin sauce. Pile it on top of a mountain of egg-fried rice for an easy weeknight classic.

500g boneless lamb

1 tsp bicarbonate of soda

1 egg white

75g cornflour

1 large onion

2 red chillies

4 spring onions

3cm of ginger

4 cloves of garlic

1 tbsp cumin seeds

½ tsp white pepper

10 dried Sichuan chillies ⁓ optional

vegetable oil

salt

FOR THE SAUCE

2 tbsp black vinegar ↔ balsamic

4 tbsp soy sauce

1 tbsp dark soy sauce

2–3 tbsp crispy chilli oil

1–2 tsp chilli flakes

1 tsp cornflour

Slice the lamb into thin strips across the grain. Put it in a bowl with the bicarbonate of soda, massage well, and allow to marinate for 30 minutes in the fridge. This is called velveting and makes the meat more tender. Rinse off the bicarb and pat dry. Then put the lamb into a bowl with the egg white, cornflour and a pinch of salt.

Meanwhile, cut the onion into large chunks, finely slice the red chillies and chop the spring onions into 4cm pieces. Grate the ginger and roughly chop the garlic.

Combine the black vinegar, soy sauce, dark soy, chilli oil and chilli flakes with 50ml water.

In a large wok, heat up 3cm of oil (enough to shallow-fry the lamb). Carefully add the lamb in a single layer and cook for 3 minutes, until it is crispy and cooked through. You can do this in two batches if necessary. Drain on kitchen paper.

Remove the oil from the wok, leaving behind about 2 tablespoons. Add the cumin seeds, onion, ginger, garlic, spring onions and chillies. (Add the whole dried Sichuan chillies now, if using.) Fry on a high heat for 4 minutes until charred and crispy. Add the lamb and the sauce, along with a slurry made with the cornflour and 100ml of water.

Allow the sauce to bubble and coat the lamb. Serve immediately.

SPICY

NOTE
→ *Freezing the lamb for 30 minutes before slicing will help you cut it thinner. Substitute with beef, chicken or even seitan!*

ALL I WANT IS SOMETHING …

FIERY SCOTCH BONNET LENTILS WITH CRISPY SALMON

SPICY

My national dish series has been one of the biggest inspirations for my recipes, and this is a take on Nigeria's iconic jollof rice. It's an incredibly spicy tomato-based rice flavoured with the mighty Scotch bonnet. These tiny yet fiery peppers pack not only intense heat but also remarkable depth and even a hint of floral notes. I've transformed lentils into a rich and spicy sauce reminiscent of jollof rice and crowned them with a crispy, succulent salmon to balance the heat, finishing with a drizzle of fresh spring onion oil.

FOR THE LENTILS

1 large onion, finely chopped

2 large beef tomatoes (about 400g)

5cm ginger, grated

6 cloves of garlic, chopped

1 Scotch bonnet pepper, chopped

1 red pepper, chopped

½ tsp allspice ···· optional

3 tbsp tomato purée

200g green lentils ↔ red split lentils

1 tsp salt

olive oil

FOR THE SPRING ONION OIL

50ml vegetable oil

4 spring onions, finely chopped

5cm ginger, finely chopped

FOR THE SALMON

4 salmon fillets ↔ any other fish or protein

1 tsp curry powder

1 tsp salt

vegetable oil

Sauté the chopped onion in plenty of oil for 5 minutes, until golden.

Meanwhile, blend the tomatoes, ginger, garlic, Scotch bonnet, red pepper and allspice, if using, using a handheld blender, until smooth.

Add the tomato purée to the sautéed onion and cook for 5 minutes, until it darkens. Add the blended tomato mixture, cook for 5 more minutes until it bubbles, then add the lentils, salt and 500ml of water. Cook on a medium heat for 30 minutes, until the lentils are tender, adding more water if needed.

Meanwhile, to make the spring onion oil, heat the vegetable oil in a small saucepan until sizzling. Add the spring onions and ginger to a heatproof bowl and carefully pour over the hot oil. Mix and season with a pinch of salt.

Rub the salmon all over with the curry powder and salt. Heat a stainless steel pan over a high heat and add a generous amount of oil. Let it heat up, then add the salmon and cook skin side down for 3 minutes. Flip and cook for 2 more minutes, until the salmon is tender and cooked through.

To serve, place the hot lentils on plates, top with the crispy salmon and drizzle over the spring onion oil.

NOTES

→   To get perfectly crispy salmon skin without sticking, cook the salmon skin side down on a piece of baking paper. Super crispy skin and no sticking!

→   If you have it, throw ½ teaspoon of allspice into the lentils for a spicy warmth!

→   Cut the cooking time in half by using pre-cooked green lentils. Use half the tomato sauce ingredients, add the cooked lentils and simmer for 10 minutes.

→   You can leave the salmon out entirely and serve the spicy lentils with rice as a comforting dal.

ALL I WANT IS SOMETHING …

PEANUTTY SALSA MACHA NOODLES

There are endless variations of chilli oil all over the world, and one of my favourites is Mexican salsa macha. With smoky dried chillies, nuts, seeds and an abundance of garlic, this is really something special. Here I've combined it with one of my favourites, Chinese dan dan noodles, using its spicy nutty sauce with fried mince, to make this incredibly moreish bowl.

400g pork mince   ↔ any minced protein

½ tsp salt

1 tsp cornflour

vegetable oil

FOR THE SALSA MACHA

100ml vegetable oil

6 cloves of garlic, roughly chopped

3 ancho chillies (or substitute, see Notes), deseeded and stems removed

3 tbsp peanuts   ↔ cashews, almonds or macadamias

1 tbsp chilli powder

3 tbsp sesame seeds

FOR THE ANCHO SAUCE

1 ancho chilli, deseeded and stems removed   ↔ see notes

2 cloves of garlic

2 tbsp soy sauce

1 tbsp oyster sauce

1 tbsp tomato purée

TO SERVE

400g round wheat noodles   ↔ other wheat noodles

4 tbsp peanut butter   ↔ any nut butter

4 tbsp soy sauce

4 tsp dark soy sauce   ⌁ optional

2 limes

4 spring onions, finely sliced

First make the salsa macha. Heat the oil in a saucepan. Add the garlic, anchos, peanuts, chilli powder and sesame seeds, and cook on a medium-low heat for 10 minutes, until the garlic is golden.

Transfer to a heatproof bowl and let it cool slightly, then blend in a food processor to form a chunky salsa.

To make the ancho sauce, bring 100ml of water to the boil in a saucepan. Add the ancho chilli, garlic, soy sauce, oyster sauce and tomato purée. Boil for 5 minutes, then blend in a food processor or using a hand blender.

Mix the pork and salt with the cornflour. Put a pan on a high heat, add a glug of vegetable oil and the pork, and cook until crispy (about 6–8 minutes). Add the blended ancho sauce and cook for 5 minutes, until thick and sticky.

Meanwhile, cook the noodles according to the packet instructions and drain, reserving the cooking water.

Divide the peanut butter, soy sauce and dark soy between four serving bowls. To each bowl add 1–2 tablespoons of salsa macha, the juice of half a lime and 2 tablespoons of cooking water (from the noodles), and top with the noodles, pork and spring onions. Enjoy!

NOTES

→ *If you find a store-bought salsa macha, just use that here to make these noodles in no time! You can also use ready-minced chicken, or any other minced protein here too.*

→ *This recipe makes more of the salsa macha than you will need, but it will keep really well in a sealed jar in the fridge for up to a month and is delicious drizzled over breakfast eggs, adding to a lunchtime toastie or for zhuzhing up a salad.*

→ *If you can't find whole ancho chillies, substitute dried chipotles or guajillos – you can play around with whatever Mexican chillies you find, but just check how spicy they are! If you use chilli flakes, substitute 1 teaspoon of flakes for 1 whole chilli.*

CHILLI PANEER V8

This Indo-Chinese classic is ordered every single time I enter an Indian restaurant. It's the perfect mix of Indian and Chinese food, and my family have very strong opinions about how it should be made. This has been in the works for the past five years and it's the best version yet – even my mum said so!

SPICY

FOR THE PANEER

2 tbsp plain flour

2 tbsp cornflour

1 tsp chilli powder

½ tsp salt

300g paneer, cut into cubes

1 tbsp vegetable oil, plus more for frying

FOR THE SAUCE

2 large red onions, 1 finely chopped, 1 in chunks

4cm ginger, finely chopped

7 cloves of garlic, finely chopped

4–6 green chillies, finely chopped   ↔ jalapeños

1 tsp chilli powder

1 tsp cumin seeds

4 tbsp soy sauce

2 tbsp tomato ketchup

2 tbsp sriracha   ↔ your fave chilli sauce

½ tsp sugar

1 tbsp rice vinegar

1 green bell pepper, cut into chunks

½ tsp five-spice   〜 optional

½ tsp salt

½ tsp ground white pepper

2 spring onions, finely chopped

Combine the plain flour, cornflour, chilli powder and salt in a small bowl.

Toss the paneer in 1 tablespoon of oil in a medium bowl, then pour in the flour mix. Freeze the paneer for 30 minutes.

Pour enough oil to shallow-fry the paneer into a large wok. Heat the oil to medium, then add the paneer in a single layer and fry for 2–3 minutes, until golden and crisp on all sides. Transfer the paneer to a sheet of kitchen paper.

Wipe out the wok with kitchen paper, then add a couple of glugs of fresh oil and return the wok to the heat. Add the onion, ginger, garlic, chillies, chilli powder and cumin seeds to the wok and cook for 5 minutes, until softened.

Meanwhile, combine the soy sauce, ketchup, sriracha, sugar and vinegar with 200ml water. Add to the wok and bring to a bubble.

Add the paneer, green pepper, five-spice, salt and pepper. Toss well and allow to heat through for 4–5 minutes, adding a splash more water if necessary to get your preferred thickness of sauce.

Taste for seasoning, then sprinkle with the spring onions and serve on its own or with rice.

NOTE

→   Freezing the paneer makes it extra soft inside, but skip this step if you don't have time.

ALL I WANT IS SOMETHING …

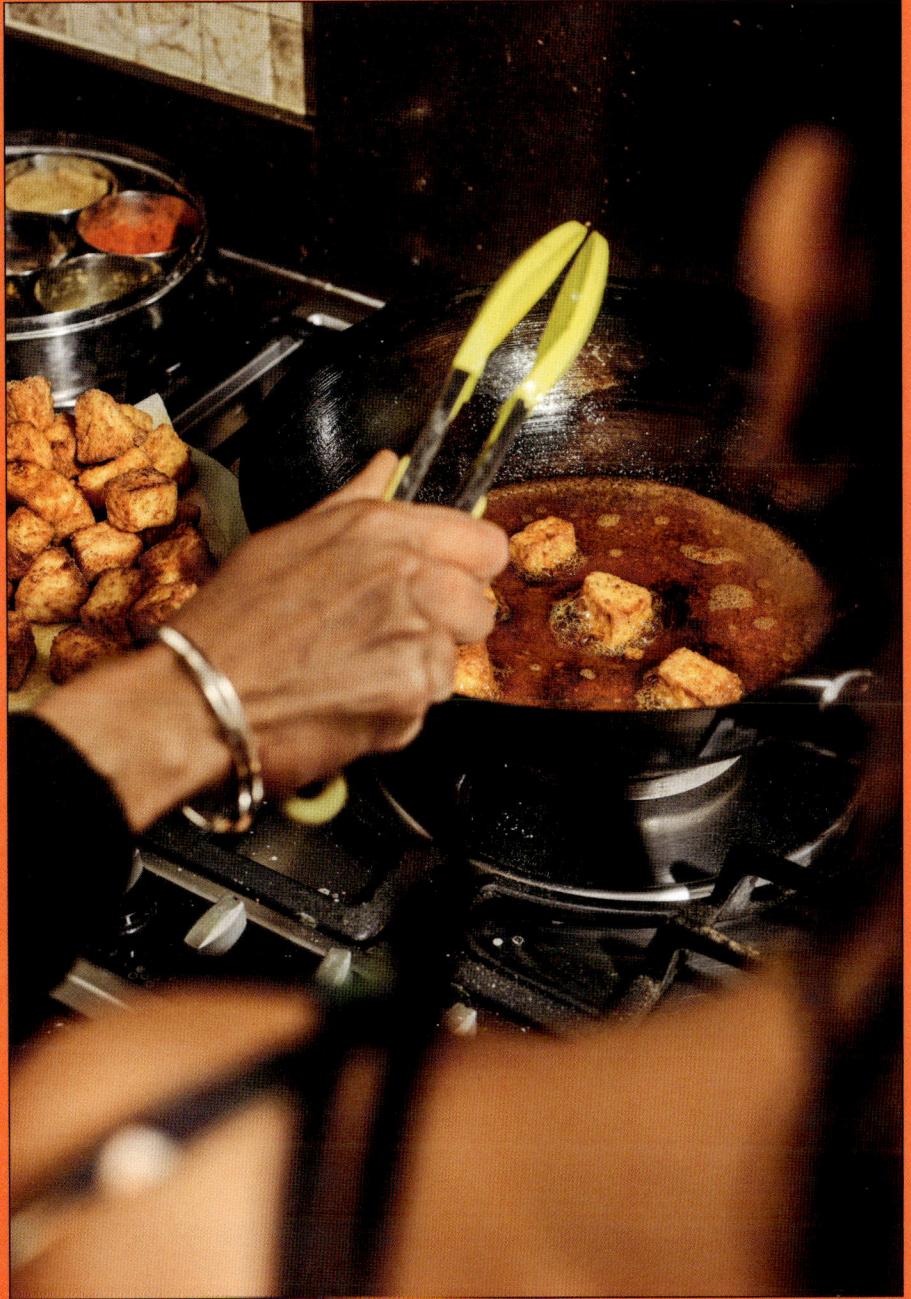

KERALAN EGG SHAKSHUKA

Keralan egg curry is a fantastically simple South Indian curry of hard-boiled eggs simmered in a spicy coconut sauce. The sauce itself is enriched by the sweetness of caramelized onions, along with coconut milk to mellow out the fiery heat. I've taken that sauce and used it as the base for this shakshuka, making it perfect with a soft jammy egg and crusty bread on lazy weekends.

Try serving this with rice for a jammy egg curry!

3 tbsp coconut oil ⟷ vegetable oil

2 large onions, thinly sliced

½ tsp fennel seeds ⟷ cumin seeds

3 green chillies, roughly chopped

4 cloves of garlic, roughly chopped

3cm ginger, roughly chopped

1 x 400g tin of tomatoes

1 tsp chilli powder

1 tsp garam masala, plus extra for sprinkling

200ml coconut milk

3–4 eggs

salt and black pepper

TO SERVE

crusty bread

1 lime

Melt the coconut oil in a heavy-bottomed pan. Add the sliced onion, fennel seeds and a big pinch of salt. Cook for 15–20 minutes, until the onions are caramelized and jammy.

Meanwhile, pound together the green chillies, garlic and ginger in a pestle and mortar – alternatively, grate or finely chop them.

Add the green chilli paste to the pan and cook for 5 minutes, until fragrant. Add the tinned tomatoes and the spices and cook for a further 20 minutes, until the sauce is very thick. Add the coconut milk and bring to a bubble.

Make some wells in the sauce and crack the eggs into the holes. Put a lid on the pan and allow it to very gently bubble for 6–7 minutes, until the whites are set but the yolks are still a bit runny.

Serve with crusty bread, a squeeze of lime and a final sprinkling of garam masala over the top.

SMASHED KEBAB BURGERS

In our household, the closest we came to a Sunday roast was our regular dinners at Taste of Pakistan in Hounslow, where we would indulge in their incredible chapli kebabs. These kebabs are known for being thin, juicy and perfectly spiced – which made me wonder how I haven't already put them in a burger. It took a bit of trial and error to get the correct flavours without compromising on the crispiness – just make sure you press down hard! They're filled with charred peppers for that 'mixed grill' feel, and melty cheese for the ultimate lamb burger.

4 burger buns, sliced in half

1 large onion, finely sliced

1 green pepper, finely sliced

2 tsp cumin seeds

750g fatty lamb mince

4 green chillies, finely chopped

1 clove of garlic, grated

½ tsp grated ginger

1 tsp chilli powder

1 tsp coriander seeds

1 tsp cumin seeds

1 tsp ground black pepper

8 slices American cheese

1 large tomato, thinly sliced

sea salt

FOR THE GARLIC BUTTER

3 tbsp butter

3 cloves of garlic, grated

1 tbsp chopped fresh coriander

¼ tsp salt

FOR THE CHILLI CORIANDER MAYO

a large handful of fresh coriander, finely chopped

3 green chillies, finely chopped

juice of 1 lemon

100g mayonnaise

To make the garlic butter, mix the butter, garlic, coriander and salt in a bowl. Brush the garlic butter over the cut side of the buns.

Put the onions and green peppers into a bowl with 1 teaspoon of cumin seeds and ¼ teaspoon of salt.

To make the burgers, combine the minced lamb, green chillies, garlic, ginger, chilli powder, coriander seeds, cumin seeds and black pepper in a bowl. Mix very gently and divide into 8 balls.

Cut out two square pieces (10 x 10cm) of baking paper (you can reuse them!).

Get your largest cast-iron pan hot and toast the garlic burger buns until golden. Then drizzle the pan with oil and heat until smoking hot. Get ready a flat-bottomed pan that will fit inside the cast-iron one.

Place one lamb ball in the cast-iron pan, sprinkle generously with sea salt, place a square of baking paper on top and smash down as hard as you can, using the second pan. Repeat with the other lamb balls and remove the baking paper. Cook for 2 minutes – when you see moisture on the top of the lamb, scrape the bottom with a metal spatula and flip.

Cook for another 2 minutes. Add a slice of American cheese on each patty and cover with a lid for 1 minute to allow the cheese to melt. Repeat with the other patties.

Tip the onion and pepper mix into the hot pan and cook on high for 5 minutes, until caramelized.

To make the mayo, whisk the coriander, chillies, lemon juice and a pinch of salt into the mayonnaise.

Spread the mayo on the base of the bun. Place the pepper mix on the bottom, top with the tomato and then burger patties (two burgers per bun), add the top bun and enjoy.

SCOTCH BONNET COCONUT BROTH & CRISPY HALLOUMI NOODLES

SPICY

Scotch bonnet peppers are among my favourite chillies to use, as they bring an abundance of flavour without the need for many other ingredients. These peppers are incredibly spicy, with a slight floral aroma, making them perfect for soups. When paired with creamy coconut milk, they create a delicious and warming broth that feels like it's been cooking for hours.

1 red onion, roughly chopped

8cm ginger, roughly chopped

6 cloves of garlic, roughly chopped

1 tsp curry powder

1 Scotch bonnet pepper, roughly chopped

2 tbsp tomato purée

400ml coconut milk

4 tbsp plain flour

2 eggs, beaten

200g desiccated coconut ⟷ breadcrumbs

400g halloumi, cut into small cubes

400g instant ramen noodles

200g pak choi, halved

a small handful of fresh coriander, finely chopped

2 limes

vegetable oil

salt

Blend the red onion, ginger, garlic, curry powder and Scotch bonnet in a food processor to create a chunky paste.

Heat some oil in a pan and sauté the paste for 10 minutes, until fragrant. Stir in the tomato purée and cook for an additional 5 minutes, until it darkens in colour.

Pour in the coconut milk, add 500ml of water, and bring to a gentle simmer.

Prepare three bowls with plain flour, beaten egg and desiccated coconut. Season each bowl with a pinch of salt.

Heat enough oil in a saucepan for shallow-frying. Dredge the pieces of halloumi in the flour, then egg, then coat them with desiccated coconut. Fry the halloumi pieces until they are golden brown, crispy and cooked through, about 3 minutes on either side.

Cook the noodles in boiling water according to the packet instructions. Cook the pak choi in the same water for 3 minutes.

Place some cooked noodles in each serving bowl, pour over the coconut broth, and top with the crispy halloumi, pak choi and a sprinkling of chopped coriander. Squeeze lime juice over each bowl and serve.

ALL I WANT IS SOMETHING …

NOTE
→ You can substitute the halloumi with crispy chicken, or tofu for a vegan-friendly version.

AIR FRYER FRIENDLY
→ Coat the halloumi with a spritz of oil and air fry at 180°C for 10–15 minutes, until it turns crispy and golden.

KOREAN-ISH FRIED POPCORN CHICKEN

This iconic sticky and spicy sauce is inspired by one that was developed in the trenches of my first (and last) food truck event with Mob Kitchen, where people queued for over two hours just for a taste of a Korean fried chicken burger. I've taken the same sauce, developed it some more, and slathered it on crispy fried chicken for the perfect bite. I opted for sour cream here instead of the conventional mayo, because when mayo gets heated it can split, but this sauce stays luscious, with a tang to cut through the fattiness of the chicken.

FOR THE CHICKEN

500g boneless chicken thighs

200g sour cream   ↔ yoghurt

1 tsp gochujang

1 tsp apple cider vinegar

1 egg, beaten

150g cornflour

150g plain flour

enough vegetable oil for deep-frying

salt

FOR THE SPICY SAUCE

5 spring onions, finely chopped

3cm ginger, grated

3 cloves of garlic, grated

200g sour cream

100g gochujang

2 tbsp soy sauce

2 tbsp crispy chilli oil with bits (we used Lee Kum Kee)

1 tbsp apple cider vinegar

1 tbsp honey

Cut the chicken into bite-sized pieces and put them into a bowl with the sour cream, gochujang, apple cider vinegar and the egg. If you like, you can leave it to marinate for 30 minutes or up to overnight, to tenderize the chicken.

For the spicy sauce, mix the spring onions, ginger and garlic with the sour cream, gochujang, soy sauce, crispy chilli oil, apple cider vinegar and honey.

Pour enough frying oil into a pan to deep-fry the chicken, and heat to around 175°C.

Combine the cornflour and plain flour in a bowl and season generously with salt. One by one, coat the chicken pieces in the flour, scrunching them with your hands to make them craggy – this will make the chicken extra crunchy.

Deep-fry the chicken for 4–5 minutes, until golden brown and crispy, and cooked all the way through – cut a piece in half to check.

Toss the fried chicken in the spicy sauce, and serve hot.

NOTES

→   Feel free to use chicken breast for something leaner, but it is less forgiving when frying, so can dry out. You could even make this with tofu!

→   I used sour cream for the chicken marinade instead of yoghurt for tenderization, so you don't have to deal with half a tub of sour cream in the fridge, but you can use a combination, or just yoghurt if that's what you have!

SPICY

ALL I WANT IS SOMETHING …

SOMETHING GREEN

SMOKY CAULIFLOWER & PEPPER SHAWARMA BOWL

When I feel like I'm craving a lot of vegetables, roasting them with loads of spices makes a really simple but super-satisfying dinner. This is my take on the iconic halal guy's cart in New York, covered with sauces but also lots of vibrant veg. It's all about balance, eh?

1 head of cauliflower, chopped into florets

1 red bell pepper, sliced

1 x 400g tin of chickpeas, drained

3 cloves of garlic

2½ tsp smoked paprika

2 tsp ground cumin

2 tbsp dried oregano

350g basmati rice

½ tsp ground turmeric

FOR THE SAUCE

100g thick Greek yoghurt

100g mayonnaise

juice of 1 lemon

1 tsp ground black pepper

½ tsp salt

2 cloves of garlic, grated

TO SERVE

4 white pita

½ a head of lettuce, chopped

1 cucumber, chopped

1 large tomato, chopped

1 red onion, thinly sliced

a small handful of fresh parsley, roughly chopped

sriracha ↔ your favourite hot sauce

Preheat the oven to 200°C.

Cut the pita into triangles and toss with 1 tbsp oil and ½ tsp smoked paprika.

On a baking tray, combine the cauliflower, bell pepper and chickpeas. Grate the garlic over the top, add the spices, oregano, 1 teaspoon of salt and 3 tablespoons of olive oil. Rub the spices into the cauliflower well and bake for 25–30 minutes, until the cauliflower is cooked through.

Wash the rice and put it into a pan. Add water to the pan, filling to about 5cm above the rice, add the turmeric and 1 teaspoon of salt, and bring to the boil. Once boiling, turn the heat to low, put a lid on the pan and set a timer for 10 minutes. Drain the rice and put it back into the pan with the lid on. Allow to steam until you're ready to eat.

Combine the ingredients for the white sauce and add 3–4 tablespoons of water to thin it down if needed.

Serve the rice in bowls, with the roasted veg, lettuce, cucumber, tomatoes, red onion, parsley and pita. Generously drizzle with the white sauce and sriracha and serve.

> ### COOKING RICE
> When I cook rice, I don't bother measuring the water. Just fill up the pot so it covers the rice, at least 5cm, cook for 10 minutes and then drain all the water when it's done. Make sure to let the drained rice steam in the pot with the lid on to get it extra fluffy!

ALL I WANT IS SOMETHING ...

AUBERGINE & MUSHROOM ISKENDER

On all my many trips to Berlin, my absolute favourite thing to eat was the iskender from Doyum, an incredible Turkish grillhouse (if you haven't tried this, please do!). Layers of crispy bread and spicy tomato, drizzled with lots of butter, usually topped with juicy lamb. I've got juicy mushrooms and aubergines in my recipe. All the veg and the croutons are roasted at the same time, so it comes together to make a very delicious weeknight meal. And if the length of the ingredients list is putting you off, I've used the same three spices several times, so it's not as many different ones as it seems!

1 large aubergine, cut into large chunks

250g mushrooms, halved

1 tsp garlic powder

½ tsp cumin seeds

1 tsp smoked paprika

1 tsp chilli powder

1 tsp salt

1 tbsp olive oil

2 tomatoes

FOR THE BREAD

300g stale crusty bread, torn into large chunks

1 tbsp olive oil

1 tsp garlic powder

FOR THE TOMATO SAUCE

2 cloves of garlic

½ tsp cumin seeds

1 x 400g tin of tomatoes

1 tsp chilli powder

1 tsp smoked paprika

1 tsp za'atar   ↔ ½ tsp sumac and ½ tsp sesame seeds

1 tsp salt

olive oil

FOR THE YOGHURT

4 spring onions, finely chopped

1 bunch of fresh parsley, finely chopped, plus extra to serve

300g thick Greek yoghurt

1 lemon

TO ASSEMBLE

50g butter

2 cloves of garlic

1 tsp smoked paprika

2 tbsp flaked almonds

a squeeze of lemon juice

pickled chillies

Preheat the oven to 200°C.

Put the aubergine and mushrooms into a bowl and add the dried spices, salt and 1 tablespoon of oil. Place them on a baking tray along with the whole tomatoes and roast for 30 minutes, tossing halfway through, until crispy and charred.

Meanwhile, put the pieces of bread on another baking tray. Drizzle with a tablespoon of olive oil and sprinkle with the garlic powder, then roast in the oven for 15 minutes, or until golden and crisp.

To make the tomato sauce, heat a glug of olive oil and add the garlic and cumin seeds. Cook for 2 minutes, then add the tinned tomatoes, chilli powder, smoked paprika and za'atar. Simmer for 15 minutes, then blend with a hand blender. Season with salt.

Mix the spring onions and parsley with the yoghurt, the juice of a lemon and ½ a teaspoon of salt. Add 2–3 tablespoons of water to loosen slightly.

To assemble, lay the croutons on your serving dish and top with the roasted veg. Layer the tomato sauce and yoghurt on top. Heat the butter in a small pan and grate in the garlic. Add the smoked paprika and flaked almonds, bring to a bubble, then when the almonds are slightly browned, pour over the dish.

Sprinkle with more parsley and a squeeze of lemon, and serve with the roasted tomato and pickled chillies.

NOTE

→   *Sub in courgettes, or even lamb or chicken pieces roasted in the same spices.*

SUMAC & LIME OYSTER MUSHROOMS

This recipe is quite a special one. It's the last recipe I put in this book and it's only in here because I had a breakdown and wanted to reshoot the cover (days before the cover was due) and this recipe was the only one that would work for the vision I had, and so it was. I've had so many different versions of these mushrooms by now and they just keep getting better and better.

3 tsp garlic powder

1 tbsp sumac

1 tsp salt

½ tsp sugar

150g flour

3 eggs

200g panko breadcrumbs

250g oyster mushrooms

zest of 1 lime

a small handful of parsley, finely chopped

vegetable oil

peri peri sauce, to serve

Combine the garlic powder, sumac, salt and sugar in a small bowl.

Get a large pot of oil heating on medium-high heat, ready for deep-frying.

Place your flour in a bowl, crack the eggs in another, and fill the third bowl with the panko breadcrumbs. Season them all with salt.

Dunk the mushrooms in flour and then the eggs and finally press on the panko breadcrumbs.

Deep-fry the mushrooms for 3 mins until golden brown and crispy.

Toss them in the garlic and sumac salt, grate on lots of lime zest on both sides of the mushroom and sprinkle with parsley.

Eat whilst still hot and enjoy the beautiful crunch

NOTES

→   Use sumac from a Middle Eastern store, good-quality sumac makes a world of a difference. You can also switch up the seasoning to match whatever meal you're having.

→   Instead of the garlic and sumac mixture, try a mixture or Parmesan, garlic powder and parsley or even some of the secret spice mix from my recipe for Seema's Fried Chicken (page 165).

CABBAGE DUMPLINGS

Dumplings and cabbage rolls are a universal love language. Fillings wrapped in parcels can be found in cuisines all over the world – whether it's sarmale from Romania, kåldolmar from Sweden, or fagottini di verza from Italy, they are hard to resist. After eating numerous versions for my national dish series, here I've combined cabbage rolls with my love of dumplings. It's a simple yet deeply satisfying meal, brimming with hearty vegetables.

    Feel free to make this dish completely vegetarian by swapping the chicken mince for crumbled tofu or using your favourite minced protein. You can also toss in any finely minced veggies, such as spinach, carrots or celery. It's the perfect way to clear out your fridge.

1 Chinese ↔ Savoy cabbage
or Napa cabbage   or white cabbage

FOR THE FILLING

200g mushrooms, finely chopped

4 spring onions, finely chopped

300g chicken mince (preferably thigh)

4 cloves of garlic, grated

3 tbsp soy sauce

½ tsp chilli flakes

1 tbsp oyster sauce

1 tbsp Shaoxing wine ↔ dry sherry, white wine or mirin

1 tbsp cornflour

salt and pepper

FOR THE DIPPING SAUCE

3 cloves of garlic, grated

1 spring onion, finely chopped

1 tbsp chilli powder

1 tbsp sesame seeds

100ml vegetable oil

2 tbsp soy sauce

1 tbsp black Chinese vinegar ↔ balsamic vinegar

Start by bringing a large pan of salted water to the boil. (This is the same pot you'll use for your steamer.) Peel the larger leaves off the cabbage, but keep the middle core with the small leaves for later. Boil the cabbage leaves for 1 minute, then remove from the water and rinse with cold water. Keep the hot water in the pan for later.

    Finely chop the core of the cabbage and combine with the rest of the filling ingredients. Heat a little oil in a small frying pan and cook 1 tablespoon of the filling. Taste and adjust the seasoning if needed.

    Lay the cabbage leaves out on a work surface. Place 1 tablespoon of the filling on a leaf and roll it up like a burrito, folding in the sides. Continue with the rest of the cabbage leaves.

    Put the cabbage rolls into a bamboo steamer lined with baking paper and steam for about 15 minutes, or until the filling is fully cooked.

    To make the sauce, put the garlic and spring onions into a bowl and add the chilli powder and sesame seeds. Heat the vegetable oil until it starts smoking. Add the garlic mixture and immediately turn off the heat. Stir well to ensure the garlic cooks evenly. Remove from the heat and add the soy sauce and vinegar.

    Serve the cabbage rolls with the sauce poured over and enjoy with steamed short-grain rice.

NOTES

→   *Don't have a bamboo steamer? Put a small bowl upside down in a large pan. Add just enough water to cover the bowl and place a plate that fits inside the pot on top. Line the plate with baking paper, and use this set-up to steam your dumplings.*

→   *If you've got any oranges or similar fruits, zest some into the dipping sauce for that delightful zing.*

GREEN

ALL I WANT IS SOMETHING …

JERK-SPICED BUTTER CAULIFLOWER & CRUNCHY MAPLE CHICKPEAS

I've always found cauliflower quite a tricky beast. I love the look of a whole roasted cauliflower, but the flavourless inside makes me a bit sad. So I've torn off large florets and rubbed every crevice with my spicy jerk butter. This packs a big punch, so don't miss out the lemony yoghurt underneath and the sweet maple chickpeas.

1 whole cauliflower, cut into quarters, stem intact

1 x 400g tin of chickpeas, drained

3 tbsp desiccated coconut

3 tbsp maple syrup   ⟷ honey

½ tsp salt

300g coconut yoghurt   ⟷ plain yoghurt

1 lemon

FOR THE JERK BUTTER

3 spring onions, roughly chopped

1 onion, roughly chopped

6 cloves of garlic, chopped

6cm ginger, chopped

2 tsp dried thyme   ⟷ rosemary   ⟿ optional

3 tsp ground allspice

2 tbsp white wine vinegar   ⟷ apple cider vinegar

3 tsp maple syrup   ⟷ honey

½–1 Scotch bonnet chilli

½ tsp ground cinnamon

50g butter

2 tbsp soy sauce

1 tsp salt

Preheat the oven to 180°C.

To make the jerk butter, blend all the ingredients until smooth, using half the Scotch bonnet to start with. Give it a taste and add more Scotch bonnet a little at a time until you get the desired spiciness.

Put the cauliflower on a baking tray and rub it liberally with the jerk butter, focusing on the florets. Roast for 30 minutes, until cooked all the way through, basting every 10 minutes with the butter and making sure the cauliflower is well coated.

Combine the chickpeas with the desiccated coconut, maple syrup and salt. Roast in the oven for 20 minutes, until crispy, stirring halfway through.

Mix together the yoghurt and lemon juice.

Serve the buttery cauliflower on top of the yoghurt, with the crispy chickpeas alongside.

NOTE

→   *Try serving this in a wrap or on thick flatbreads with a quick coleslaw.*

CARAMELIZED RED ONION & COURGETTE ORZO SALAD

There is a phrase, what grows together goes together, and that's very true for courgette and corn. Both are charred until blistered – times when I love my gas hob – and tossed with a really zesty sumac and caramelized onion dressing. The dressing is a nod to the flavours of glorious musakhan, the national dish of Palestine. There, chicken is bathed in a slowly cooked sea of onions, then generously dusted with more sumac than you'd think is appropriate. Yet it all comes together incredibly beautifully, just like this salad.

3 courgettes

2 cobs of corn

250g orzo

200g frozen peas

a small handful of fresh mint, roughly chopped

50g feta cheese

salt and black pepper

FOR THE DRESSING

2 red onions, thinly sliced   ↔ any onions

50ml extra virgin olive oil

4 cloves of garlic, finely chopped

½ tsp chilli flakes

2 tbsp sumac   ↔ 2 tbsp za'atar and zest of 1 lime

juice of 2 lemons

1 tsp honey

½ tsp ground cumin

Put the onions into a heavy-bottomed pan with the extra virgin olive oil and a large pinch of salt, and cook for 20 minutes on a medium heat until jammy and caramelized. Set aside.

Meanwhile, cross-hatch the courgettes and rub them with salt. Char the courgettes and corn on a grill pan until the courgettes have softened and the corn is charred, about 10 minutes. You can also use your gas hob, gently rotating them on the flame or under a very hot grill.

Chop the courgette into chunks and slice the corn off the cobs.

Boil the orzo according to the packet instructions, adding the peas for the last 2 minutes of cooking.

Return the pan of onions to a low heat and add the garlic, chilli flakes and sumac. Cook for 2 minutes, then take off the heat and add the lemon juice, honey and cumin. Toss the dressing with the cooked veg, orzo and mint, then crumble in the feta and adjust the seasoning.

GREEN

ALL I WANT IS SOMETHING …

STICKY UMAMI MUSHROOM RICE BOWL

Does mushroom count as a vegetable? Anyway, one of my ultimate comfort foods is buttery soy sauce rice. Trust me, hot rice with a salted butter and soy sauce is insanely delicious. I've kept the umaminess of butter and soy and topped it with some crispy charred mushrooms for an incredibly satisfying bowl of rice. Then it's all fused together with a creamy egg yolk for some extra richness.

FOR THE RICE

3 spring onions, roughly chopped	
2 shallots, finely chopped	
6 cloves of garlic, roughly chopped	
4cm ginger, grated	
400g sushi rice	↔ any short-grain rice
500ml vegetable stock	
2 tbsp Shaoxing wine	↔ dry sherry, mirin or sake
1 tsp salt	
vegetable oil	

FOR THE STICKY MUSHROOMS

50g butter	
1 tbsp oyster sauce	↔ veggie oyster sauce
4 tbsp soy sauce	
400g oyster mushrooms	
200g firm tofu, cut into small cubes	
1 tsp cornflour	
2 tsp sesame oil	
4 egg yolks	

Preheat the grill to its hottest setting.

Melt the butter in the microwave and combine in a large bowl with the oyster sauce, soy sauce and 100ml of water.

Add the oyster mushrooms and tofu to the bowl and massage them well so they absorb some of the liquid.

Reserve some of the spring onions for garnish and put the rest into a heavy-bottomed pan with the shallots, garlic, ginger and a large glug of oil. Fry for 5 minutes, until softened.

Wash your rice until the water runs clear. Add the rice to the pan with the shallots, along with the stock, Shaoxing wine and salt. Bring to a bubble, then turn the heat to low and put a lid on. Allow to cook for 15 minutes, then turn off the heat and let the rice steam for 10 minutes.

Meanwhile, place the mushrooms and tofu on a baking tray, reserving the liquid, and grill for 25–30 minutes, or until charred. Set aside.

Put the reserved mushroom liquid into a small pan and bring to a boil. Make a slurry with the cornflour and 2 tablespoons of water, then add to the mushroom liquid to thicken. Toss the mushrooms and tofu in the liquid and remove the pan from the heat.

Divide the sticky mushrooms and tofu between the bottoms of 4 serving bowls and fill the rest of the bowls with rice.

Turn the bowls upside down on to a plate, to unveil the mushroom domes. Brush with sesame oil and top each one with an egg yolk and the chopped spring onions and enjoy.

NOTE

→   Use whatever mushrooms you have. If they are chestnut or button mushrooms, tear them up with your hands so they get more crispy. But as a treat, oyster mushrooms have a meatiness that works fantastically here!

CRUNCHY COCONUT & SESAME BROCCOLI

Any time I need a quick green side for any meal, this is always my go-to. It goes with everything, looks quite special and tastes fantastic. The simple sesame sauce is based on a traditional Japanese goma sauce, using tahini as a quick hack. And the crunchy coconut topping is inspired by the many coconut chutneys I had in Kerala. You can even cheat and just mix toasted coconut into your favourite chilli crisp – I promise not to tell anyone!
This is great as a quick lunch over rice.

500g broccoli, thick stems sliced in half lengthways

FOR THE SESAME SAUCE

4 tbsp tahini	↔ 2 tbsp of any nut butter
4 tbsp rice vinegar	↔ white wine vinegar
1 tsp soy sauce	
2 tsp brown sugar	
1 tsp sesame oil	
5 tbsp hot water	

FOR THE CRUNCHY COCONUT TOPPING

2 tbsp peanuts, roughly chopped

2 tbsp desiccated coconut

50ml vegetable oil

1 tbsp chilli flakes

2 tbsp fried shallots

salt

Cook the broccoli in heavily salted boiling water for 4–5 minutes, until tender.

Meanwhile, combine all the ingredients for the sesame sauce. When you add the water it will start to clump up, but continue whisking in more water until it's a smooth sauce. Season with ¼ teaspoon of salt.

Roughly chop the peanuts and toast in a pan with the desiccated coconut until golden. Add the vegetable oil and chilli flakes. Once the chilli flakes start to fizz, cook for a further 30 seconds and then turn off the heat. For the shallots, slice thinly then toss lightly in flour and fry in a little oil until crispy. Transfer the peanuts, coconut and and shallots to a bowl and add ½ teaspoon of salt.

Lay the broccoli on a plate and drizzle over the sesame sauce. Sprinkle with the crunchy coconut and serve.

NOTES

→ Cook your broccoli whichever way you want – keep it simple by just boiling or steaming, roast it in a fiery hot oven, or blanch it quickly in water and char it on a hot pan.

→ I'm using premade fried shallots/onions, which I always keep in my pantry, but if you want to make your own, you can thinly slice them and fry them in a few tablespoons of oil until golden and crispy.

→ This works great for any green veg! Try it with some pak choi or just lots of wilted spinach.

ALL I WANT IS SOMETHING …

THAI BASIL AUBERGINE

Herbs are far more than just a garnish, and recipes like this really showcase them. This recipe is all about celebrating the herbal glory of basil. You'll want to use enough basil so that it takes centre stage in your dish, much as you would with spinach.

This creation draws inspiration from fiery Thai basil chicken, a super-spicy and fragrant dish, but I've used caramelized onions to mellow out the heat from those fiery peppers.

GREEN

Ingredients	
4 tbsp olive oil	
2 large aubergines, chopped into 5cm chunks	
3 small onions, sliced	
5 cloves of garlic, finely chopped	
3 Thai red chillies (small ones), finely minced	↔ 4 long red chillies or 1 tsp chilli flakes
3 tbsp soy sauce	
1 tbsp oyster sauce	↔ veggie oyster sauce
200g cherry tomatoes, halved	
2 large handfuls of Thai basil (about 100g), leaves picked	↔ regular basil
salt	

Heat 2 tablespoons of oil in a wok over a medium heat and fry the aubergines on all sides until they turn a glorious golden colour. Once done, remove from the wok and set aside.

Add 2 more tablespoons of oil to the wok. Toss in the onions and let them cook slowly for 20 minutes, until they become soft and wonderfully caramelized.

Stir in the garlic and chillies, letting them sizzle for another 2 minutes.

Return the aubergines to the wok, and add the soy sauce, oyster sauce, cherry tomatoes and 100ml of water. Let it all bubble together for 15 minutes, allowing the sauce to thicken and the aubergines to become tender. If things look a bit dry, add a splash of water.

Finally, add the basil leaves and toss until they wilt. Season with a pinch of salt and serve on a bed of fluffy rice.

NOTE

→ When working with hot chillies, it's best to blend them or use a pestle and mortar to avoid any unexpected bursts of spicy heat in your mouth. If you prefer a milder kick, go for just two long red chillies.

ALL I WANT IS SOMETHING . . .

ALL I WANT IS...

SOMETHING COMFORTING

CITRUSY MISO ROAST CHICKEN WITH PICKLED CHILLI & CHIVE DRESSING

Roast chicken has always been one of my favourite things on the planet, and in this recipe, which takes inspiration from Ottolenghi's miso butter onions, the miso gives it a buttery, savoury boost and the citrus cuts through the richness. When it was topped with the vinegary dressing, my brother said it was the nicest roast chicken he'd had.

1 whole chicken

200g shallots, ↔ white onions, halved peeled and left whole

500g baby new potatoes

50g butter

1 orange, cut into wedges, to serve

1 lime, cut into wedges, to serve

FOR THE MARINADE

juice of 1 orange

juice of 2 lemons

juice of 1 lime 〰 optional

6 cloves of garlic, crushed

2 tbsp brown sugar

2 tbsp miso paste

1 tbsp dried tarragon ↔ sage or oregano

1 tbsp coriander seeds, crushed

FOR THE PICKLED GREEN CHILLI & CHIVE DRESSING

1 bunch of fresh chives, ↔ spring onions finely chopped

2 tbsp sesame seeds

3 green chillies, roughly chopped

½ tsp salt

3 cloves of garlic, chopped

50ml vegetable oil

2 tbsp rice vinegar ↔ apple cider vinegar

Preheat the oven to 220°C (this may seem high, but spatchcocked chicken cooks much faster).

Using a pair of kitchen scissors, cut the backbone out of the chicken. Flip it over and press firmly on the breast to flatten the chicken, then turn out the legs so they are facing outwards.

For the marinade, put the citrus juice into a large bowl. Add the garlic, brown sugar, miso paste, tarragon and coriander seeds.

Place the chicken in the marinade, skin side down, and optionally leave to marinate for 30 minutes to 1 hour, but no longer, as the citrus can start to cure the chicken.

Place the shallots and potatoes on a large baking tray and dot with knobs of butter. Put the chicken on top of the potatoes and pour the marinade over the top.

Roast in the oven for 45 minutes, spooning the marinade over every 15 minutes.

Once the chicken is cooked and the juices run clear, remove from the oven and place on a chopping board. Leave to rest for 15 minutes. Meanwhile, return the potatoes and shallots to the oven for a further 15 minutes to crisp up.

To make the dressing, place the chives in a heatproof bowl and set aside.

Pound the chillies, salt and garlic in a pestle and mortar.

Toast the sesame seeds in a small pan until golden, then add the oil to the sesame seeds along with the pounded garlic mix. Allow to sizzle for 2 minutes, then pour over the chives in the bowl and stir in the rice vinegar.

Once the chicken has rested, slice it into thighs, legs, wings and breast. Serve on top of the potatoes and shallots with the tangy chive mix spooned over and orange and lime wedges alongside for squeezing over.

COMFORTING

127

ALL I WANT IS SOMETHING …

FRENCH ONION GNOCCHI

When it comes to winter soups, French onion soup reigns as the undisputed king. The slow caramelization of the onions is a labour of love in itself, resulting in a deep, rich flavour that's worth every minute. In this recipe, those beautifully caramelized onions are paired with tender gnocchi, all swimming in a hearty stock infused with the umami goodness of miso and earthy mushrooms. It's the kind of comforting meal that warms you from the inside out.

Make this completely veggie by leaving out the Worcestershire sauce.

Ingredient	Substitution
250g chestnut mushrooms, sliced	
500g onions, thinly sliced	
1 vegetable stock cube	
1 tbsp miso	⌇ optional
1 tbsp Worcestershire sauce	↔ use 1 anchovy, or omit
1 tbsp balsamic vinegar	↔ white wine vinegar or red wine vinegar
6 cloves of garlic, finely chopped	
4 tbsp butter	
½ tsp dried thyme	↔ dried rosemary
150ml dry white wine	↔ chicken or vegetable stock, plus 2 tbsp white wine vinegar
500g potato gnocchi	
100g Gruyère cheese	↔ any melty cheese
50g panko breadcrumbs	
50g Parmesan, grated	↔ veggie Parmesan or other hard cheese
olive oil	
salt	

In a dry pan over medium heat, cook the mushrooms with a pinch of salt for about 10 minutes. The water in the mushrooms will evaporate first, and once they're dry and start sticking to the pan, add 1 tablespoon of olive oil and cook for an additional 3 minutes on a high heat until crispy. Transfer them to a bowl.

Using the same pan (no need to clean it), cook the onions with a generous amount of oil on a medium heat for 25 minutes, until they are very caramelized. Add a tablespoon of water if the pan looks dry and continue cooking.

Preheat the oven to 180°C.

Crumble the vegetable stock cube into a bowl and add the miso, Worcestershire sauce and balsamic vinegar. Stir in 500ml of boiling water to dissolve the stock cube.

Finely chop the garlic and add it to the onions along with the butter and thyme. Cook for 2 minutes, then deglaze with the white wine. Bring to a simmer, then add the vegetable stock mixture, cooked mushrooms and the gnocchi. Stir and cook for 10 minutes, until the sauce thickens.

Grate half the Gruyère and roughly chop the rest. Mix the roughly chopped cheese into the pan of gnocchi.

Transfer the gnocchi mixture to a baking dish and cover it with the breadcrumbs, the grated Gruyère and the Parmesan. Bake for about 15 minutes, or until it turns golden and crispy.

COMFORTING

129

ALL I WANT IS SOMETHING …

CHEAT'S CURRIED OMURICE

If you've fallen down the rabbit hole of TikTok and witnessed the glorious cascading scrambled egg pocket, chances are you've encountered the legend himself, Chef Motokichi Yukimura, the Omurice maestro from Kichi Kichi Omurice. It fuelled my obsession, but despite how easy he makes it look, it's not. And so that you don't need to feel my disappointment, I've developed a cheat's version that gets you 85 per cent there with 10 per cent of the fuss. Then it's all smothered in a quick curry sauce that hits all the spots without the heartache.

FOR THE CORIANDER SPRING ONION RICE

300g rice

1 vegetable stock cube   ↔ chicken stock cube

2 spring onions, finely chopped

1 tsp dark soy sauce

a small handful of fresh coriander, finely chopped

FOR THE CURRY SAUCE

1 carrot, grated

1 onion, grated

1 tsp grated ginger

2 cloves of garlic, grated

1 tsp curry powder

½ tsp garam masala   ⸺ optional

½ tsp chilli powder

1 tbsp plain flour

2 tbsp soy sauce

1 tbsp honey

vegetable oil

salt

FOR THE EGGS

4 eggs

2 tbsp butter

Wash the rice three times until the water runs almost clear, then drain.

Dissolve the chicken stock cube in 300ml of water.

Put the rice into a pan with the spring onions, chicken stock and soy sauce. Bring to a simmer, then turn the heat to low, put a lid on and cook for 10 minutes. Once cooked, allow to rest for 5 minutes, then mix in the chopped coriander.

To make the curry sauce, heat a glug of oil in a pan and add the carrot, onion, ginger and garlic. Sauté for 5 minutes, until softened.

Add the curry powder, garam masala and chilli powder and cook for 2 minutes. Stir in the flour and cook for 2 minutes, then slowly pour in 400ml of water, mixing well.

Add the soy sauce and honey, and bring to a bubble. Season with salt.

To cook the eggs, place the smallest non-stick frying pan you have on the lowest heat setting. Crack in 2 eggs (you must do this one serving at a time) and add the butter. Very gently scramble together on a low heat, using a spatula to make soft-set eggs. Fold the eggs over each other, making small curds. Once the eggs are three-quarters cooked, turn off the heat and allow the bottom to set slightly.

To serve, fill a bowl with the rice and tip it upside down on to a plate to make a dome. Place the egg on top of the dome, and ladle over the curry sauce.

NOTES

→   If you can find those Japanese curry blocks, you can use 2 cubes instead of the spices, flour and honey for a rapid curry sauce.

→   This is great for using up leftover rice – you can stir-fry it with garlic and spring onion, or double up on the egg for an egg-fried rice!

FEEL BETTER GINGER & LIME CHICKEN SOUP

My ultimate comfort food is always soup. It's warming, comforting and has this undeniable power to wrap you up in a blanket. For when you're not feeling too well, I've developed this simple soup that will get you back in action in no time. It also works great frozen without the pasta, so you can have it ready for some really sniffly emergencies.

1 onion, finely chopped

1 carrot, finely chopped

5 cloves of garlic, finely sliced

6cm ginger, half grated, half finely chopped

½ tsp ground turmeric

1 tsp whole black peppercorns

1 tsp whole coriander seeds   ↔ try cumin seeds instead!

1 whole chicken   ↔ 4 bone-in chicken thighs

½ a cabbage

250g small pasta (I keep alphabet pasta for emergencies)   ↔ egg noodles

2 green chillies (jalapeños), chopped

1 bunch of spring onions, chopped

a small handful of fresh coriander, chopped

juice of 2 limes

vegetable oil

salt

4 tbsp full-fat yoghurt, to serve

Heat a big glug of vegetable oil in a large stockpot. Add the onion, carrot, garlic and the grated ginger. Sauté for 3 minutes, then add the turmeric, black peppercorns, coriander seeds and your whole chicken. Pour in cold water so that the chicken is covered. Bring to a simmer and allow to cook on a low heat for 45 minutes.

Remove the chicken from the pan and shred the cooked meat, discarding the bones (or for an extra chickeny broth, see notes).

Roughly chop the cabbage and add it to the soup. Cook for 10 minutes. Cook the pasta according to packet instructions.

Meanwhile, combine the chopped ginger, green chillies and most of the spring onions and coriander in a heatproof bowl. Heat up 50ml of vegetable oil and pour this over the spring onion/ginger mix. Squeeze in the lime juice, then taste and season generously with 1 teaspoon of salt.

Plate up your soup with pieces of chicken, cooked pasta, sprinkle with the reserved coriander and spring onions, dollop over the yoghurt and spoon over the spring onion oil.

NOTES

→   *For an extra intense chickeny flavour, roast the bones with a bit of oil at 200°C, until dark golden, then put them back in the soup to simmer for another hour.*

→   *I love how the yoghurt adds some freshness to the soup, but you can also use a drizzle of cream if yoghurt's not your thing.*

ONLY COMFORTING

ALL I WANT IS SOMETHING …

CREAMY PAPRIKASH BEANS

I'm always intrigued by the simplicity of staple home dishes around the world. Hungarian paprikash is no exception, the star of the show being their beloved paprika flavouring a thick chicken stew. Hungarian paprika is far superior to our supermarket version, but I've used the essence of the dish to make these delightfully creamy beans, perfect for scooping with crusty bread.

This would be great paired with crunchy roasted potatoes (try my garlicky anchovy butter smashed potatoes on page 56).

1 onion, finely chopped

1 red bell pepper, finely chopped

5 cloves of garlic, finely chopped

1 tsp chilli flakes

2 tbsp tomato purée

2 tbsp smoked paprika

1 tbsp apple cider vinegar

100ml double cream

1 x 400g tin of butter beans

olive oil

salt and ground black pepper

TO SERVE

50g feta

a small handful of fresh basil

½ tsp chilli flakes

4 slices of crusty bread

Sauté the onion, red pepper, garlic and chilli flakes with a glug of oil in a pan for 10 minutes, until soft.

Add the tomato purée and cook for a further 5 minutes, until darkened. Add the smoked paprika, apple cider vinegar, double cream and the beans, including the liquid from the tin.

Mix well and bring to a bubble, then allow to cook for 5 minutes until warmed through and thick. Season generously with salt and pepper.

To serve, crumble over the feta and scatter over the basil leaves and chilli flakes. Drizzle with olive oil and enjoy with slices of crusty bread.

COMFORTING

135

ALL I WANT IS SOMETHING …

SEB'S TARRAGON CHICKEN

One of the most comforting foods for me is chicken, and this chicken is one of the best I've had. Seb made it for me when I first visited his family home in Sweden – he picked all the herbs from his mum's garden, grilled the chicken on their woodfire grill and packed it with garlic just the way I like. The way to my heart is chicken, and I hope this chicken makes its way into yours.

a large handful of fresh tarragon, finely chopped

3 cloves of garlic, finely chopped

a small handful of fresh oregano, finely chopped   ↔ parsley, chives or thyme

1 lemon

50ml extra-virgin olive oil

½ tsp salt

1 tsp coarse ground black pepper

4 chicken thighs, skin on

TO FINISH

2 cloves of garlic, finely sliced

2 tbsp butter

Put 2 tablespoons of the chopped tarragon into a large bowl, along with the chopped garlic, the oregano, the juice of ½ a lemon, 50ml of olive oil, salt, black pepper and the chicken thighs.

Marinate for 20 minutes (optional, or while you heat the grill, if using).

Heat a cast-iron skillet on a medium heat. Brush off most of the marinade from the chicken thighs (reserving it for later) and cook them skin side down for 7 minutes, until golden and crisp.

Turn the chicken over and continue cooking for 4–5 minutes. Remove and allow to rest on your serving plate.

Meanwhile, finely slice the rest of the garlic.

Add the reserved marinade, sliced garlic and butter to the pan and cook for 2 minutes, until fragrant. Turn off the heat and mix in the remaining tarragon.

Pour the buttery tarragon mix over the chicken. Squeeze over the juice of ½ a lemon, sprinkle with flaky sea salt, and serve.

NOTES

→   *This is a perfect summer BBQ recipe: grill the chicken on the grate and cook the marinade with the butter in a pan. Serve with some grilled potatoes to soak up the butter.*

→   *If you want to get fancy and make for easier eating, debone the chicken – make sure to reduce the cooking time by half if you do so.*

ALL I WANT IS SOMETHING ...

ONLY COMFORT

MISO MUSHROOM CARBONARA-ESQUE SPAGHETTI

Creamy mushroom pasta has always been my favourite, but there are just never enough mushrooms for me, and the addition of cream can make the pasta feel too heavy. So I've loaded this recipe with mushrooms, so you really get a mouthful per bite. The meatiness of the mushrooms plus a dash of miso paste makes this veggie 'carbonara-style' pasta, where I use the egg yolks and Parmesan to make a lusciously creamy sauce.

300g mixed mushrooms

½ tsp chilli flakes

½ tbsp black pepper, plus extra to serve

250g spaghetti

75g Pecorino, plus extra to serve   ↔ veggie pecorino or other hard cheese

3 egg yolks

1 tbsp white miso paste

6 cloves of garlic, thinly sliced

extra virgin olive oil

salt

Tear the mushrooms into a large dry pan with ½ a teaspoon of salt and cook for 10 minutes, until all the water has evaporated and the mushrooms start to brown. Add a large glug of oil, the chilli flakes and black pepper, and brown the mushrooms for 5 minutes.

Cook your spaghetti in a large pan of lightly salted boiling water according to the packet instructions, and drain, reserving the cooking water and returning it to the pan over a medium heat.

Grate the pecorino using the star side of the box grater – or blitz to dust. This makes it easier to melt it into the sauce. In a heatproof bowl, whisk the pecorino, egg yolks and miso paste with 125ml of pasta cooking water.

Add another glug of oil to the mushroom pan. Add the garlic and cook for 5 minutes, then add a splash of pasta water to stop it cooking.

Turn off the heat and add the cooked spaghetti and the egg yolk mixture. Place the bowl over the boiling pasta water and mix vigorously until it's all emulsified, adding more pasta water as needed to make a thick glossy sauce.

Serve with more grated pecorino and black pepper.

ONLY COMFORT

ALL I WANT IS SOMETHING …

CRISPY CHILLI GARLIC ROAST POTATOES

I'm not the biggest fan of potatoes – they need to be perfectly crispy and saucy so that I don't get that stodgy feeling in my throat. These potatoes are wonderfully crisp, and tossed in an Indo-Chinese-style sticky sauce. Indo-Chinese is the melding of Indian and Chinese food, using the savouriness of soy sauce with the rich Indian spices. They would go great with any spicy main, or just as is, dunked in some yoghurt.

1kg potatoes, peeled and cut into large chunks

50ml vegetable oil, plus 2 tbsp ⟷ ghee

1 tbsp plain flour

1 large onion, finely chopped

8 cloves of garlic, finely chopped

2 tsp chilli powder

1 tsp ground coriander

1 tsp ground cumin

6 tbsp ketchup

6 tbsp soy sauce

200g thick Greek yoghurt

1 tbsp chopped fresh coriander

Preheat the oven to 200°C.

Pop your potatoes into a pan of salted cold water, bring to the boil, and cook for 15 minutes, or until just fork tender.

Meanwhile, pour 50ml of vegetable oil on to a large baking tray and place it in the oven to heat for 10 minutes.

Drain the potatoes and put them back into the pan. Add 1 tablespoon of flour, then put the lid on the pan and shake to fluff them up.

Take the hot baking tray out of the oven and immediately pour the potatoes on to it so they sizzle. Toss the potatoes in the oil and put them back into the oven for 45 minutes, turning halfway, until they are very crispy.

For the sauce, put the onions and garlic into a pan with 2 tablespoons of oil and fry for 5 minutes, until soft and translucent. Add the chilli powder, ground coriander and cumin and cook for 1 minute. Mix in the ketchup and soy sauce and turn off the heat.

Once the potatoes are crispy, toss them with the chilli sauce and serve with the yoghurt and sprinkled with the fresh coriander.

COMFORTING

ALL I WANT IS SOMETHING …

ZA'ATAR RICOTTA DUMPLINGS

Ricotta gnudi are a beloved Italian comfort food, and my twist on these soft, pillowy dumplings takes them to another level. They're coated in a za'atar Parmesan sauce and drizzled with a fresh, zesty zhoug-like dressing. (Zhoug is a spicy cardamom and coriander dressing from Yemen!) You can whip up this delightful dish in less than 30 minutes, making it perfect for any busy weeknight.

FOR THE RICOTTA GNUDI

250g ricotta	
160g plain flour, plus extra for rolling	
1 egg	
50g Parmesan, grated	↔ veggie Parmesan or other hard cheese
2 tbsp za'atar	
1 tsp salt	
½ tsp freshly ground black pepper	

FOR THE ZHOUG-LIKE DRESSING

a large handful of fresh parsley

2 green chillies

1 tbsp za'atar

juice of ½ a lemon

50ml extra virgin olive oil

FOR THE PARMESAN SAUCE

1 shallot, finely chopped	
2 tbsp butter	
6 cloves of garlic, thinly sliced	
150ml white wine	↔ chicken or vegetable stock
100ml double cream	
50g Parmesan, grated	↔ veggie Parmesan or other hard cheese

Strain the ricotta by pressing it in a sieve over a bowl to remove the excess water.

In a mixing bowl, combine the strained ricotta, flour, egg, Parmesan, za'atar, salt and pepper. Mix to form a slightly sticky dough.

Place a few tablespoons of plain flour in a bowl. Roll small balls of dough in your hand, coat them in the flour and make an indentation with your thumb in the middle. Use more flour if needed. Repeat with the rest of the dough and arrange the gnudi on a floured baking tray.

Bring a large pot of lightly salted water to the boil.

For the zhoug-like dressing, blend the parsley, green chillies, za'atar and lemon juice, and slowly drizzle in the olive oil while blending until you have a smooth dressing. Set aside.

In a saucepan, cook the shallot with the butter for 5 minutes, until softened. Add the garlic and cook for 2 more minutes. Deglaze with the wine and bring to the boil. Stir in the double cream and Parmesan, then reduce the heat.

Drop the gnudi into the boiling water and cook until they float to the surface, about 1 minute. Transfer them to the Parmesan sauce, toss together and add some cooking water if the sauce is too thick.

Serve the gnudi with the spicy zhoug-like dressing and a drizzle of olive oil.

NOTES

→ Try out other spice mixes, such as ras el hanout or even Old Bay seasoning, if you don't have any za'atar.

→ Raid your fridge for any extra herbs such as basil or coriander to toss into the dressing. If you happen to have some olives on hand, they'd also make a fantastic addition.

ALL I WANT IS SOMETHING…

COMFORTING

PICKLED JALAPEÑO MAC & CHEESE

Mac and cheese is universally known as comfort food. I've combined it with one of my other comforts, cheesy jalapeño nachos from the cinema – making this one of the greatest things you can eat while watching a movie in bed. The secret is the one and only plastic cheese, which gives it that signature flavour. Generously topped with crispy onions, because you deserve it.

Ingredient	Substitution
500g macaroni	↔ any short pasta shape
50g butter	↔ vegetable oil
50g plain flour	
750ml milk	↔ oat milk
200g mature Cheddar, grated	↔ any cheeses you have
100g red Leicester, grated	
5 American cheese slices (the more processed, the better)	
100g pickled jalapeños, finely chopped	↔ any pickles from the fridge
100ml pickling liquid from the jalapeño jar	
salt and pepper	

FOR THE TOPPING

Ingredient	Substitution
50g tortilla chips, crushed	↔ breadcrumbs
50g crispy shallots	
50g Parmesan cheese, grated	↔ veggie Parmesan or other hard cheese

Preheat the oven to 180°C.

Cook the macaroni in lightly salted boiling water for about 10 minutes, or a few minutes less than the recommended cooking time on the packet. It will finish cooking in the sauce in the oven.

Melt the butter in a large saucepan and stir in the plain flour. Cook this mixture for about 2 minutes. Then slowly drizzle in the milk in three additions, making sure to whisk well after each addition.

Add the grated Cheddar and red Leicester, and the slices of American cheese, and mix until all the cheese has melted. Add the cooked pasta, chopped jalapeños and the pickling liquid. Stir everything together and season with salt and pepper.

Pour the cheesy pasta mixture into a baking dish and top it with the crushed tortilla chips, crispy shallots and a generous sprinkle of grated Parmesan.

Bake for 20 minutes, or until it's golden and bubbling. Allow to rest for 5 minutes, and enjoy.

NOTES

→ Be sure to check the net weight of the jar of jalapeños!

→ When it comes to cheese, let your creativity run wild. This recipe is fantastic for using up those little remnants hiding at the back of your fridge. Start with mature Cheddar as your base and throw in whatever other cheeses you have on hand. It's all about making it your own!

COMFORTING

ALL I WANT IS SOMETHING …

PEA & POTATO CURRY

A home classic for me is potato and pea curry. It's a dish you wouldn't normally see being served in Indian restaurants, but that's how you know it's one of the good ones. For me there are always peas in the freezer and potatoes somewhere in the cupboard. The curry takes less than 30 minutes to make and is one of the most comforting meals on a cold day. Have this with rice or rotli.

8cm ginger, roughly chopped

7 cloves of garlic, roughly chopped

200g tinned tomatoes (whole or chopped)

½ tsp cumin seeds

2 tsp chilli powder

1 tsp ground cumin

1 tsp ground coriander

¼ tsp ground turmeric

500g potatoes, peeled and cut into small chunks

200g frozen peas

1 tsp salt

vegetable oil

a small handful of fresh coriander, to serve

Blitz together the ginger, garlic and tinned tomatoes.

Heat a large glug of oil in a pan and add the cumin seeds. Once they start to sizzle, pour in the blended tomato sauce.

Add the chilli powder, ground cumin, ground coriander, turmeric and salt, and mix well.

Add the potatoes, then pour in 250ml of water and let this bubble for 15–20 minutes, until the sauce is thick and the potatoes are cooked through.

Add the peas, and finally squish some of the potatoes against the side of the pan to thicken the curry. Cook for another 5 minutes.

Finish with the chopped coriander and serve.

CHAAS (SALTY LASSI)

Every meal at my mum's was not complete without chaas (salty lassi). It's salty, savoury and perfect with any curry. Simply whisk together 150g yoghurt, 200ml cold water, 1/4 teaspoon roasted and crushed cumin seeds and 1/4 teaspoon of salt.

LEFTOVERS

→   *If you have leftovers, this makes the best toastie filling ever! Pile it up on some bread with some cheese and coriander chutney for a fantastic lunch!*

ROTLI

Rotli is something I am very fussy about. They need to be hot, soft and very thin. Try one freshly cooked with lots of butter and you will understand my fussiness. My mum's recipe means they stay soft for days – her secret is to use hot water. Chapati flour also helps the rotlis puff up in that iconic ball, but if you don't have any, use wholemeal or even plain flour.

300g chapati flour, wholemeal or plain

pinch of salt

1 tbsp vegetable oil

200ml boiling water

Combine the chapati flour with a pinch of salt, 1 tablespoon of oil and 200ml of boiling water straight from the kettle. Mix it with a spoon until it's cool enough to handle, then knead for 5 minutes to form a sticky dough. Pour 1 tablespoon of oil over the dough and continue to knead so that the dough is less sticky and very soft.

Cover the dough and allow it to rest for 15–20 minutes.

Place a frying pan on a high heat and allow it to warm up for 2 minutes.

Pinch off a golfball-sized piece of dough and liberally dust your work surface with flour. Roll the dough gently into a small circle and coat it again with flour. Continue rolling until you form a thin circle about 15cm in diameter.

Place the rotli face side down in the frying pan. Cook for 30 seconds, until small bubbles appear, and then flip it. Cook for a further 30 seconds and flip again. Then, using a clean tea towel, press down on the rotli. This will help it to puff up – press down on the parts that are puffing up to push the air to the sides of the rotli.

While one rotli is cooking, roll out the next one – bring in a friend to help you. Continue rolling and cooking the rotli until you have run out of dough.

Enjoy with a curry, or even spread with butter and sprinkled with sugar as a snack.

COMFORTING

ALL I WANT IS SOMETHING…

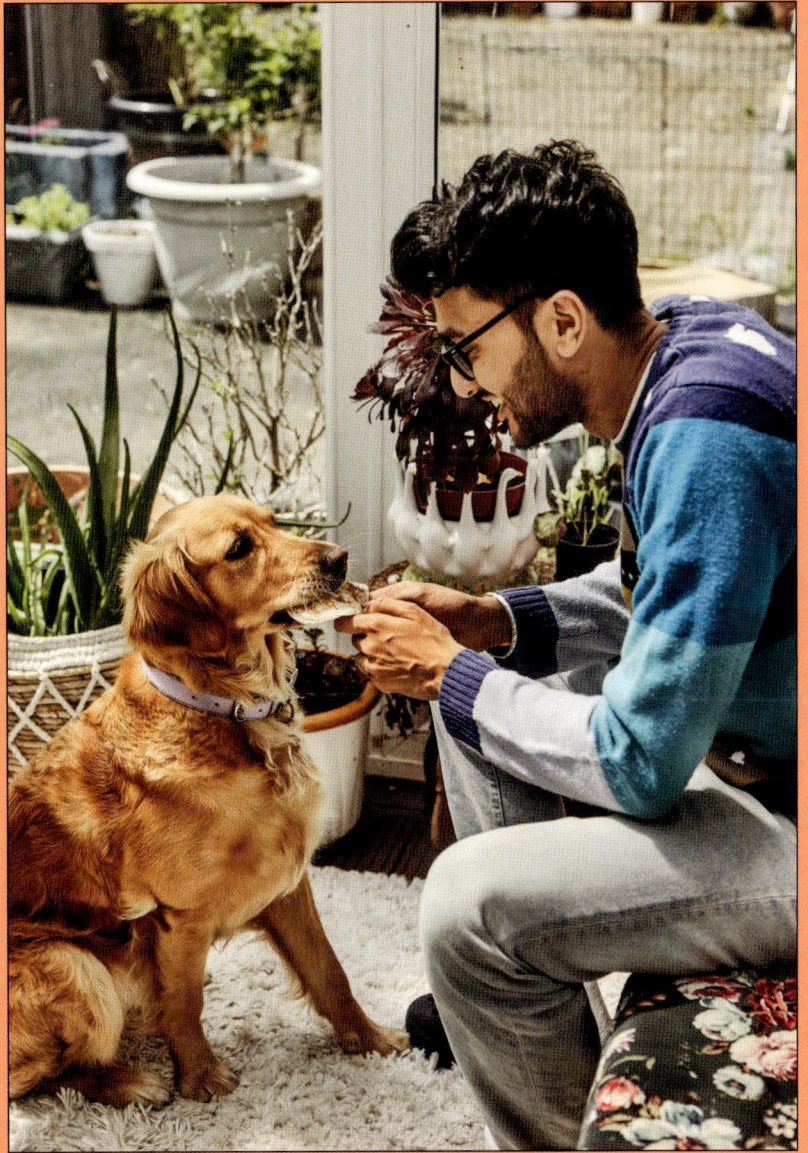

CACIO E PEPE SPÄTZLE

This is a fantastic hack for creating a dish with the feeling of homemade pasta when in fact it takes around 30 minutes. I had the idea when I was seeing Chinese scissor-cut noodles along with a German technique for making spätzle. You use this with an Italian pasta dough and then combined with an Italian sauce it will feel like fresh homemade pasta with no fuss.
It's one of my proudest creations and now you can see it all over the internet!

100g plain flour	↔ 00 flour
1 large egg	
pinch of salt	
1 tsp freshly ground black pepper	
50g pecorino cheese	↔ veggie pecorino or other hard cheese

Combine the plain flour with the egg and a pinch of salt and knead for 5–8 mins to form a soft dough. Cover with cling film and rest for 15 (and up to 30) minutes.

Bring a pot of boiling salted water to the boil.

Using a pair of clean kitchen scissors, snip very small thin pieces of the dough ball directly into the water. Allow to boil for 2–3 mins, until floating, then drain, reserving some of the pasta water.

Warm a pan over a low heat and grind in 1 teaspoon of black pepper. Toast for 1 minute, then ladle in 150ml of the reserved pasta water. Add the cooked pasta and then sprinkle over the grated cheese. Allow to sit for 30 seconds without stirring until the cheese melts, then toss the sauce and pasta together so the sauce coats the pasta.

Plate up with extra black pepper and cheese and enjoy.

NOTE
→ Use this technique to make fresh pasta for any pasta dish! I love it with a simple tomato sauce too.

SOMETHING SPECIAL

THE BUTTER CHICKEN

Of all the recipes I've ever cooked, this one holds a special place in my heart, and for good reason. This isn't your run-of-the-mill creamy, mildly sweet butter chicken. The sauce is rich, and it's got a kick that will wake you up a bit. It doesn't really fit the traditional butter chicken mould, and there isn't a cashew in sight, but that's what makes it so special. This recipe has left an indelible mark on my life and culinary journey, and it's easily what I've become best known for, so naturally it was a must-have in this book.

FOR THE CHICKEN MARINADE

150g plain full-fat yoghurt (must be full-fat!)

juice of ½ a lemon

1 tsp red chilli powder

½ tsp ground turmeric

1 tsp ground cumin

1 tsp ground coriander

½ tsp garam masala

1 tsp salt

800g boneless chicken thighs, cut into bite-sized pieces

FOR THE GARLIC, GINGER & CHILLI PASTE

10 cloves of garlic, minced or grated

a piece of ginger, minced or grated

6 green chillies, minced or grated

FOR THE CURRY

150g butter ←→ ghee

1 large onion, finely chopped

1 star anise ⁓ optional

1 cinnamon stick ⁓ optional

3–4 cloves ⁓ optional

½ tsp cumin seeds

1 tsp ground cumin

1 tsp garam masala

1 tsp ground coriander

1 tsp salt ←→ to taste

3 tbsp tomato purée

1 x 400g tin of chopped tomatoes

2 tsp red chilli powder

250ml double cream

2 tbsp dried fenugreek ⁓ optional
leaves (kasoori methi)

juice of ½ a lemon

a small handful of fresh coriander

SPECIAL

ALL I WANT IS SOMETHING…

Preheat the grill to the highest setting.

Mix together the garlic/ginger/chilli paste ingredients in a small bowl. In a larger bowl, mix all the marinade ingredients, and stir in half the garlic/ginger/chilli paste. Add the chicken and mix well. If you are making this ahead you can now cover and leave in the fridge until the next day. If not, carry on as below.

Place the marinated chicken on an oven tray and grill until it's charred, about 5–6 minutes on each side. It doesn't need to cook through at this stage.

In a large pan, melt the butter over a medium heat. Once it's melted, add the finely chopped onions along with the optional star anise, the cinnamon stick, cloves and cumin seeds. Cook the onions for about 10 minutes, until they turn golden and caramelized. Then add the rest of the garlic/ginger/chilli paste, the ground spices, salt and the tomato purée. Cook for another 10 minutes, until the tomato purée separates from the oil.

Add the tinned tomatoes and cook for 15–20 minutes, until the sauce thickens and the oil separates from the tomato mixture, creating a rich sauce.

Add the grilled chicken, along with any cooking liquid. Stir in the double cream and add the dried fenugreek leaves, if using. Stir well and cook for about 5 minutes, until the chicken is fully cooked through.

Squeeze in the juice of ½ a lemon, taste and adjust the seasoning if necessary.

Garnish with fresh coriander and serve with rice and naan bread.

NOTE

→ *Don't stress about the whole spices – they're optional. If you've got them, toss 'em in. But there's no need to make a special trip to the store. What's important, though, is to use good-quality chilli powder from the international foods aisle at your local supermarket. It really makes a difference!*

VARIATION – MAKE IT VEGGIE

→ *Swap the chicken and yoghurt for 400g of paneer or tofu and 50g of cornflour. Omitting the yoghurt, toss it with the same spices as the chicken, until well coated, then lift individual pieces of paneer or tofu into the pan and pan-fry it until it's deliciously golden. Add it to the dish at the same point you'd include the chicken.*

SERVING IDEA

→ *Serve this with buttered naan, a side of rice and some sliced red onions tossed in a lemon dressing.*

LEFTOVERS

→ *Make a quick little butter chicken toastie by layering cheese, green chutney (page 165) and leftover curry between two slices of bread and toasting until golden.*

SPECIAL

ALL I WANT IS SOMETHING …

CURRIED CABBAGE WEDGES

Cabbage is one of the most versatile and scrumptious vegetables you can find. It offers a savoury, slightly sweet taste, and is so moreish. This fall-apart braised cabbage is incredibly simple to make, and is a mix of Thai yellow curry and Indian tarka (where spices and curry leaves are tempered in oil and poured over the top), resulting in an incredible flavour combination. Don't forget the crispy garlicky tarka – it's a must have, and if you can lay your hands on some curry leaves, even better. Be sure to serve this with a generous bowl of rice for soaking up all those delicious oils.

1 medium white cabbage, quartered

1 stalk of lemongrass

4 green chillies

3 shallots   ↔ 1 large onion

4cm ginger

3 garlic cloves

½ tsp ground turmeric

2 tbsp coconut oil

400ml coconut milk

1 lime

salt

FOR THE TARKA

2 tbsp coconut oil

6 cloves of garlic, thinly sliced

1 tsp cumin seeds

½ tsp ground turmeric

a few sprigs of curry leaves, leaves picked

Put the cabbage quarters into a bowl and salt them with ½ a teaspoon of salt.

Heat an ovenproof pan and drizzle with a little oil. Sear the cabbage on all the cut sides until they turn golden brown. Set aside.

Preheat the oven to 200°C.

Bash the lemongrass with the handle of a knife to separate the fibres, then finely chop. Blitz the green chillies, shallots, ginger, garlic, turmeric and lemongrass in a mini food processor.

Heat the coconut oil in a cast-iron frying pan and fry the chilli paste for 5 minutes until it softens. Pour in the coconut milk and add 1 teaspoon of salt. Bring to a bubble, then pour over the cabbage wedges and coat them with the sauce. Bake in the oven for 30 minutes, or until tender.

When the cabbage is almost ready, prepare the tarka. Heat the coconut oil in a small pan and add the garlic, cumin and turmeric. Cook for 3 minutes, or until the garlic starts to turn brown round the edges. Add the curry leaves and cook for 30 seconds.

Once the cabbage is cooked, use a spoon to drizzle over the crispy topping.

Squeeze the lime juice over the cabbage and serve on a bed of rice.

NOTES

→   To speed up the process, consider using store-bought yellow Thai curry paste instead of the fresh spices.

→   Unfortunately, there is no direct substitute for curry leaves. If you can't find them, it's best just to leave them out. However, I would recommend grabbing some whenever you come across them and storing them in the freezer.

ALL I WANT IS SOMETHING...

SEEMA'S FRIED CHICKEN

If I were the Colonel, this is what a family bucket would look like: crispy golden crust enveloping succulent tandoori chicken, all dusted with my (not-so-secret) special spice blend. When it comes to fried foods, I'm a firm believer in adding spice dust: it allows you to infuse incredible flavours without loading up the batter or flour. In fact, you can keep this spice blend handy in a jar and sprinkle it over just about anything.

FOR THE CHICKEN

2 eggs

200g yoghurt

juice of 1 lemon

1 tsp chilli powder

4 cloves of garlic, grated

4cm ginger, grated

2kg skin-on, bone-in chicken legs and thighs

1 tbsp spice mix

300g plain flour

FOR THE SECRET SPICE MIX

1 tbsp chilli powder

1 tbsp ground cumin

1 tbsp garlic powder

1 tsp garam masala

½ tsp black pepper

2 tbsp sugar

1 tbsp MSG   ⁓ optional

1 tbsp salt

FOR THE MASALA GRAVY

4 tbsp butter

1 onion, finely chopped

2 tbsp spice mix

2 tbsp plain flour

500ml water

2 tbsp gravy granules (I like Bisto Best chicken gravy)

FOR DEEP-FRYING

3 litres vegetable oil or enough for deep-frying

FOR THE GREEN CHUTNEY

a large handful of fresh coriander

a small handful of fresh mint

2 green chillies

50g roasted peanuts   ⁓ optional

juice of 1 lemon

100g yoghurt

SPECIAL

ALL I WANT IS SOMETHING …

Combine all the ingredients for the secret spice mix in a bowl and adjust to your taste preferences (more chilli, more garlic, etc.).

Combine the eggs, yoghurt, lemon juice, chilli powder, garlic, ginger into a large bowl and add the chicken pieces and 1 tablespoon of the spice mix. Set aside to marinate for 30 minutes. If you want to prep a day ahead, you can cover and transfer to the fridge overnight.

For the masala gravy, add the butter to a small saucepan and gently cook the onions for 10 mins until softened and caramelized. Add 2 tbsp of the spice mix, cook for 30 seconds then add in the plain flour. Whisk well and gradually add 500ml of water to make a thick gravy. When bubbling, add in the gravy granules and season to taste.

In a large pan, heat the vegetable oil to 170°C.

Pour the plain flour on to a large plate and season with salt. Dip the chicken pieces into the flour, pressing and squeezing to coat the chicken thoroughly. Repeat the process three times to create a craggy texture – this is the trick to making the chicken extra crispy!

Deep-fry the chicken pieces for 8–12 minutes, until they are golden and very crispy. Fry the legs together and the thighs together, since they cook in the same amount of time. Use a thermometer to check the internal temperature at the thickest part – it should be 72°C.

Drain the fried chicken on kitchen paper and sprinkle generously with the spice mix.

While the chicken is frying, make the green chutney by blending the coriander, mint, green chillies, peanuts, lemon juice and yoghurt together until smooth.

Serve the fried chicken with the green chutney.

NOTES

→   *While you can experiment with different spice combinations, make sure you keep the sugar, salt and MSG in the mix. This unique blend of seasonings is the secret to making fried chicken truly finger-licking good!*

→   *Plan on serving approximately one leg and one thigh per person. If you prefer boneless chicken, remember to reduce the frying time by half.*

CRISPY CHILLI GARLIC KERALA PRAWNS

Kerala has some of the most delicious fish and shellfish I've ever had, smothered in garlic and fried in coconut oil. I've been dreaming of it ever since. Seafood with Indian flavours isn't something that I grew up with, but it is incredibly popular in the south of India. Make sure you mop up that crispy garlic chilli oil with some naan. I know you're not meant to have favourites, but this may be my favourite recipe in the book!

1kg head-on and shell-on prawns (750g de-shelled)

100ml coconut oil

1 bulb of garlic, peeled and roughly chopped

2 tbsp desiccated coconut

10 long dried chillies (e.g. Sichuan chillies, De arbol chillies, but *definitely not* Thai chillies), finely chopped

1 tbsp chilli flakes (plus an extra tbsp if you like)

1 tbsp chilli powder ⸺ optional, see note

3 tbsp crispy shallots

½ tsp sugar

1 tsp salt

½ tsp MSG

10 fresh curry leaves

2 limes, cut into wedges

Remove the shells and devein the prawns, keeping the heads on – they give lots of flavour to the oil and are great to suck on.

In a large pan, melt the coconut oil and add the garlic and desiccated coconut. Cook for 5 minutes on a medium heat, until the garlic is golden brown and crispy. Turn the heat to low and add the chopped chillies and chilli flakes, chilli powder (if using), shallots, sugar, salt and MSG. Cook for a further 2 minutes, until the oils start to look red.

Add the prawns to the pan and cook for 2 minutes on each side. Before flipping them over, add the fresh curry leaves.

Toss the prawns well in the garlic and lay them out on a platter. Add some wedges of lime and enjoy with rice or hot naan.

SPECIAL

ALL I WANT IS SOMETHING …

NOTE
→   Dried chillies and chilli flakes vary a lot in heat, so try your chilli oil and add a bit more chilli powder if you want it spicier. In this recipe I use Sichuan long dried chillies, which tend not to be too spicy. And if you want to reduce the heat, remove the seeds!

SIZZLING BROWN BUTTER TANDOORI LAMB CHOPS

Every Christmas everyone waits for my cousin Mitesh's famous lamb chops. They are incredibly tender and tossed in a chilli garlic brown butter. I look forward to them every year, and I hope you enjoy them as much as I do. To make this a real feast with the lamb, there's an Indian-style tahdig with onion and peas, and of course a sour vinegary mint chutney.

1 bulb of garlic

8 green finger chillies

5cm ginger

50g yoghurt

2 lemons

½ tsp amchoor (unripe mango) powder   ↔ sumac or lime zest

1 tsp ground cumin

1 tsp garam masala

1 tsp dried fenugreek   ⁓ optional

2 tsp red chilli powder

½ tsp black pepper

1kg lamb rack, cut into chops

4 tbsp butter

2 tbsp vegetable oil

2 onions, thinly sliced

Preheat the grill to 220°C.

Remove 3 cloves of garlic from the bulb and pound them together with 4 green chillies and the ginger.

Keep the remaining cloves of garlic in their skins and slit 4 green chillies in half.

Combine the pounded garlic, chillies and ginger in a bowl with the yoghurt, the juice of 1 lemon, the amchoor and ground spices. Add the lamb chops and leave to marinate for 30 minutes or overnight.

Roast the lamb chops on a tray in the grill for 8 minutes, so they are a few minutes away from being cooked.

Meanwhile, melt the butter in a pan with 2 tablespoons of oil. Add the lamb chops, unpeeled garlic and halved chillies. Fry for 2–3 minutes on each side on a high heat until dark and caramelized.

Set aside to rest and toss the onions into the buttery pan. Cook for 5 minutes, until charred and softened.

Put the lamb chops on top of the onions and serve sizzling.

SPECIAL

NOTE
→   *Toss some rice in the pan with the lamb juices for a great chef's treat! Also note that this lamb is cooked medium rare – if you prefer it rare, reduce the grilling time to 5 minutes.*

171

CRISPY CUMIN RICE & PEAS (TAHDIG-STYLE)

400g basmati rice

2 onions, chopped

1 tsp cumin seeds

2 tbsp yoghurt

100g frozen peas

vegetable oil

Wash the rice three times, until the water runs almost clear. Then put it to soak in cold water for 30 minutes.

Bring a large pot of heavily salted water to the boil and add the rice. Cook for 5 minutes, until par-cooked, then drain.

Meanwhile, cook the onions in a pan with a glug of oil and the cumin seeds for 10 minutes.

In a bowl, combine 1 cup of rice with the yoghurt. Press this on to the bottom of a non-stick lidded pot.

Combine the remaining rice with the onions and peas, and spread on top of the yoghurt rice.

Wrap a tea towel around the lid of the pan and place the lid on securely. Cook on a medium-low heat for 25–30 minutes, until you can start to see the rice around the edges turning crispy.

Remove the lid, and (very dramatically) flip the rice on to a plate. Tap very firmly on the base of the pan to release the crispy rice.

If your rice doesn't come off in one piece, scrape it off with a spatula and arrange on a plate – it will taste just as good!

VINEGARY MINT CHUTNEY

a large handful of fresh mint

4 tbsp olive oil

2 tbsp apple cider vinegar

1 green chilli

½ tsp salt

Blend all the ingredients together and serve.

CARAMELIZED ORANGE SICHUAN BRAISED OXTAIL

When it comes to braising meat, oxtail is the underdog. It's a relatively cheap cut, packed with so much flavour, and the marrow in the middle melts into the sauce to create something really magical. I've used my favourite Jamaican oxtail stew, creating a base of dark caramel and then enriching it with Sichuan flavours and spices for a deeply rich dish. The only way to finish this off is by gnawing on the bones at the end – don't worry, no one's watching!

3 tbsp vegetable oil

1.5kg oxtail pieces

1 orange

25ml dark soy sauce

50ml light soy sauce

50ml apple cider vinegar

250ml beef stock

3 shallots, quartered

a large knob of ginger, roughly chopped

8 cloves of garlic, roughly chopped

2 tbsp white sugar

2 star anise

1 cinnamon stick

1 tsp Sichuan peppercorn powder

1 Scotch bonnet, left whole

Put 3 tablespoons of vegetable oil into a heavy-bottomed pot and place on a high heat. Add the oxtail pieces and brown them for 2 minutes on all sides, until they are deeply golden. Transfer to a plate.

Using a knife, cut the peel off the orange and set aside. Squeeze the orange juice into a jug and add the dark soy, light soy, apple cider vinegar and beef stock.

Add the shallots, ginger, garlic and sugar to the pan you browned the oxtail in. Allow to caramelize and brown for 5 minutes so the sugar melts and turns amber.

Deglaze the pan with the orange juice liquid and put back the oxtail, along with the orange peel, star anise, cinnamon stick and Sichuan peppercorn powder. Poke holes in the Scotch bonnet with a knife, leaving it whole, and add it to the pan.

Bring to a simmer, then reduce the heat to low and allow to bubble for 3 hours, or until the meat is falling-off-the-bone tender.

Serve over egg-fried rice (recipe opposite) to soak up all of that delicious sauce.

SPECIAL

NOTES

→   If you are looking for something a bit more meaty, just replace the oxtail with bone-in short ribs. Try to use something on the bone, to get more flavour.

→   If you only have whole Sichuan peppercorns, crush them in a pestle and mortar.

ALL I WANT IS SOMETHING…

EGG-FRIED RICE

Whenever I want to serve anything with fried rice, simplicity is best (this is also a fantastic way to use up leftover rice in the fridge).

3 cloves of garlic, roughly chopped

300g leftover rice

2 eggs

1 tbsp soy sauce

½ tsp salt

2 spring onions, roughly chopped

vegetable oil

Heat up a large glug of oil in a wok (pour the oil around the edge of the wok, so it falls to the centre and is evenly spread out).

Turn up the heat to high and add the garlic. Cook for 30 seconds, until fragrant, then add in the rice. Break up the rice with the back of a spoon and toss with the garlic.

Push the rice to one side and crack in the eggs. Break up the eggs and cook separately to the rice until they are scrambled.

Combine the eggs with the rice. Add the soy sauce, salt and spring onions and toss well.

SPICED CHIPOTLE SHORT RIB RAGÙ

Here, soft and buttery short rib is simmered with smoky chipotle chillies to make one of my all-time favourite slow-cooked pastas. All the spiciness and warmth of chipotle braised beef tossed through red wine and pappardelle. Every time I make this, my flat smells like the most delicious warming stew you can imagine. It's hearty, spicy and you will certainly need some soft bread to mop up every last bit left at the bottom of the bowl.

500g (net weight) jarred roasted red peppers

1kg beef short rib

1 tsp salt

1 tsp cumin seeds

1 tsp coriander seeds

1 tsp chilli flakes

150g pancetta, finely chopped   ↔ smoky bacon

1 onion, finely chopped

2 sticks of celery, finely chopped

1 carrot, finely chopped

6 cloves of garlic, thinly sliced

100g chipotle paste   ↔ dried chipotles (see notes)

250ml red wine

1 x 400g tin of chopped tomatoes

1 tsp dried oregano

750g pappardelle

olive oil

50g pecorino romano, grated, to serve

a small handful of fresh parsley, finely chopped, to serve

Finely chop half the red peppers and blitz up the rest with a handheld blender.

Pour a large glug of oil into a heavy-based pan over a high heat. Salt the short rib liberally and sear on all sides until very golden. Put on a plate and set aside.

Add another tablespoon of oil and turn the heat to medium. Add the cumin seeds, coriander seeds, chilli flakes, pancetta, onion, celery, carrot and garlic and fry for 15 minutes, until caramelized and golden.

Add the chipotle paste and fry for 3 minutes, until it has darkened slightly. Deglaze the pan with the red wine. Add the chopped peppers, blended peppers, tinned tomatoes and oregano and bring to a bubble, then add the beef. Cover with a lid and simmer for 3–4 hours, or until the meat is fork-tender and falling apart.

Remove the beef from the pan and shred with a fork. Put it back into the sauce and add 1 teaspoon of salt.

Cook the pasta until al dente, according to the packet instructions, and drain, reserving the cooking water. Add the pasta to the pan of meat sauce and combine well, adding some of the pasta water to make a thick glossy sauce.

Serve with the grated pecorino and chopped parsley.

NOTES

→   Substitute braising beef such as chuck for a cheaper alternative. You can also use lamb shoulder.

→   To make your own roasted red peppers, preheat the oven to the highest grill setting. Rub the peppers with oil and pop them under the grill for 15 minutes, or until the skin is charred – you can also do this on a gas hob or using a blowtorch. Once charred, put the peppers in a bowl with a plate over the top and leave them to steam for 15 minutes, then peel.

→   To use dried chipotles, soak 5 chipotle chillies in 150ml of boiling water for 10 minutes, then blitz up.

SPECIAL

ALL I WANT IS SOMETHING …

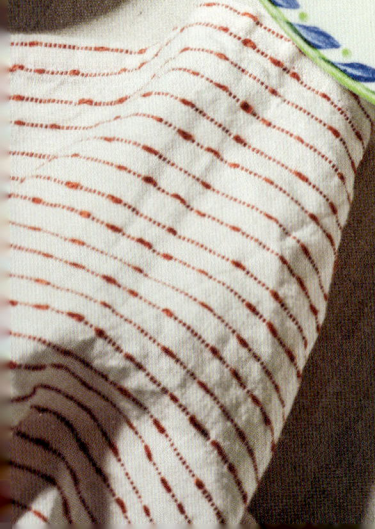

SPICY THAI-STYLE PORCHETTA

If you're looking for a main that's going to please almost everyone, this is it. Everybody gets a bit of the best part, the crackling skin, and the juicy spicy pork. It's packed full of flavour and is incredibly impressive. Dipped in a Thai-style nam jim jaew dipping sauce, which is wonderfully sour and spicy, perfect with the fatty pork belly and served with lots of rice – try subbing this for your Sunday lunch. The most tricky bit is the tying-up, but if you know how to tie your laces, you can truss up a pork belly.

1 large boneless pork belly
(ask the butcher to take the ribs off)

2 shallots, roughly chopped

1 bulb of garlic, roughly chopped

a small handful of Thai basil   ↔ regular basil

6 Thai red chillies, roughly chopped

4cm ginger, roughly chopped

1 lemongrass stalk, roughly chopped

6 makrut lime leaves

1 tsp salt

FOR THE CRISPY SKIN MIX

3 tsp salt

½ tsp white sugar

½ tsp MSG

2 tsp baking powder

FOR THE NAM JIM JAEW

2 tbsp jasmine rice   ↔ any rice

a small handful of fresh coriander, chopped

1 small shallot, finely sliced

6 tbsp fish sauce

juice of 2 limes

1 tsp brown sugar

1 tsp chilli flakes

TO SERVE

Thai basil

baby gem lettuce

SPECIAL

ALL I WANT IS SOMETHING …

Lay the pork belly flat on the work surface skin side up and slice horizontally across its width, just below the top layer of skin, until almost, but not quite, through to the other side. Open the pork belly up like a book so that the skin is now facing down. Very gently cross-hatch the meat side of the belly, being careful not to cut all the way through.

Blitz the shallots, garlic, Thai basil, Thai red chillies, ginger, lemongrass and lime leaves in a food processor to form a paste. Season with 1 teaspoon of salt. Spread this all over the entire topside of the pork (both the meat side of the pork belly and the underside of the skin layer), massaging it into the crevices made by the cross-hatching.

Using butcher's twine or kitchen string (make sure your string doesn't have plastic on it!), roll the meat up and tie tightly so that the knot is at the top. Repeat at 4cm intervals until you have a tightly tied roast.

Combine the salt, sugar, MSG and baking powder in a small bowl and liberally coat the skin of the pork. Put the meat into the fridge for at least 4 hours or ideally overnight (the longer you can leave it, the more chance you have of a crispy skin).

Once you are ready to cook, preheat the oven to 155°C. Place the pork on a wire rack in the centre of the oven and roast for 1½–2½ hours, depending on the size. After 1½ hours, check the temperature by inserting a probe in the thickest part, repeating every 30 minutes until it reaches 65°C.

Now increase the oven temperature to 230–250°C and roast for 15–30 minutes, until the skin is puffed up and crisp. Make sure to keep an eye on it. Allow to rest for 15 minutes before slicing.

For the dipping sauce, toast the rice in a small pan until golden, then place in a pestle and mortar and crush to a fine powder. Put the coriander and shallots into a bowl and mix with the rice powder, fish sauce, lime juice, brown sugar and chilli flakes. Add 4 tablespoons of hot water to dissolve the sugar and mix well.

Slice the porchetta and serve with Thai basil leaves, baby gem lettuce and the dipping sauce.

LEFTOVERS

→   *When I've had leftovers I've finely chopped the meat, fried it and had it on tacos with some salsa!*

ALL I WANT IS SOMETHING…

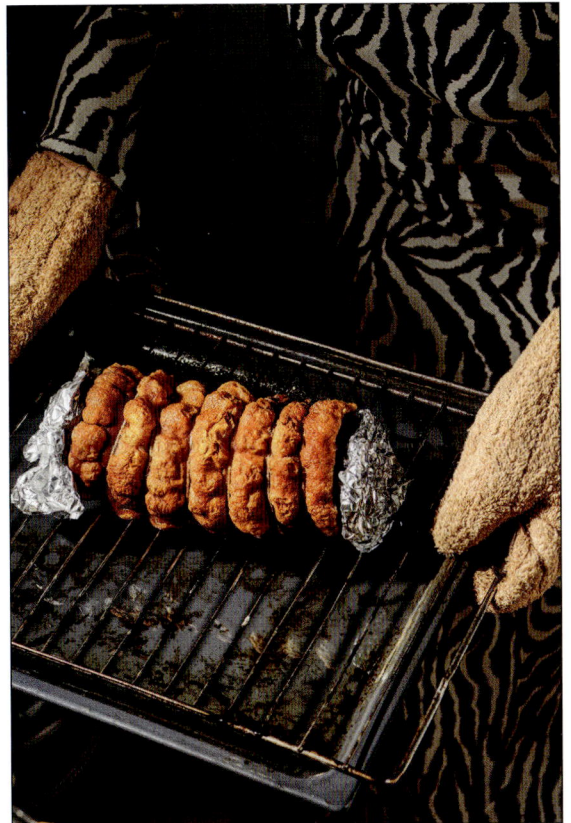

STICKY TAMARIND COLA RIBS

If you bought your pork belly for the porchetta recipe from a butcher, you are likely to have also received pork ribs. So this recipe is to pair with the porchetta, but is also fantastic if you just want some seriously simple sticky ribs.

1kg pork ribs

4cm ginger, grated

6 cloves of garlic, grated

250ml full-fat cola

2 tbsp tamarind paste

3 tbsp soy sauce

1 tbsp sugar

½ tsp fennel seeds   ⸻ optional

2 star anise

1 cinnamon stick

Preheat the oven to 155°C and place all the ribs in a roasting tray so they lie flat and snug.

Put the ginger and garlic into a small pan and add the cola, tamarind paste, soy sauce, sugar, fennel seeds, star anise and cinnamon. Place on a high heat and reduce to half.

Pour the tamarind marinade over the ribs and roast for 2 hours, until they are extremely tender and sticky.

SPECIAL

ALL I WANT IS SOMETHING …

NOTES

→   This marinade works great with chicken wings too!

→   The cola must be full-fat so you get the sugar to caramelize in the oven!

SPICY & SOUR PORK BELLY RICE

One of my kitchen indulgences is fatty, buttery rice (as seen in my gochujang steak recipe). When rice absorbs rich, luscious fats, it becomes soft, tender and irresistibly juicy. This is what I have been dreaming about. In this recipe the pork belly fat is rendered out and soaked up by the rice, and then it's all coated with a spicy sour sauce inspired by the Sri Lankan black pork curry. (I recommend you try the original from Hoppers when you can!)

500g pork belly, skin on, cut into bite-sized pieces

1 tsp sugar

2 tbsp soy sauce

2 tbsp balsamic vinegar

2 tbsp tamarind paste

3 large onions, thinly sliced

1 lemongrass stalk

6 cloves of garlic

3cm ginger

6 green chillies

15 curry leaves

1 tsp cumin seeds

1 tsp chilli powder

1 tsp garam masala

1 tbsp tomato purée

vegetable oil

salt

FOR THE RICE

400g basmati rice

2 lemons, thinly sliced

a small handful of fresh coriander, finely chopped

1 large pinch of saffron   ↔ turmeric

3 tbsp milk

NOTE

→   Replace the pork belly with chicken, lamb or beef. Reduce the cooking time to 30 minutes if using chicken.

Put the pork belly pieces into a bowl and combine with the sugar, soy sauce, balsamic and tamarind.

Put the onions into a large heavy-based pot with 50ml of vegetable oil and a big pinch of salt, and cook on a medium-high heat for 10–15 minutes until the onions are crispy. Use a sieve to drain the onions, reserving the oil. Use the back of a knife to bash the lemongrass, starting at the tip. Chop finely, and then blitz with the garlic, ginger and green chillies.

Put 2 tablespoons of the reserved onion oil back into the pot and add the curry leaves, cumin seeds and the garlic paste. Cook for 5 minutes, then add the chilli powder, garam masala and tomato purée.

Cook for 5 minutes, until the tomato purée has darkened, then pour in 200ml of water and mix well. Add the pork belly with its marinade, three-quarters of the crispy onions and 1 teaspoon of salt. Mix well and bring to a simmer.

Turn the heat to low and allow to bubble for 2 hours, lid ajar. The pork should be buttery soft and fork tender, with a thick sauce. Skim 3 tablespoons of fat off the top, or more, depending on how fatty the meat was. Taste and adjust the seasoning, and add more tamarind if you want it more sour.

Meanwhile, wash the rice three times, until the water runs almost clear. Then soak the rice in cold water for 30 minutes.

Once the pork is almost done, bring a large pan of heavily salted water to the boil and add the rice. Cook for 5 minutes, then drain – you are only parcooking the rice.

Rub the bottom of a large heavy-based pot with oil and layer in half the rice. Layer over the pork belly and half the lemon slices. Top with the remaining rice, lemon slices, the coriander, crispy onions and pork fat. Grind the saffron and allow to steep in warm milk for 5 mins. Then sprinkle the saffron milk over the rice. Wrap the lid with a tea towel and cover the rice.

Put the heat on to medium, and when you can see steam, turn it to low and allow to steam for 20 minutes.

Turn the heat off and allow to stand for 10 minutes before serving.

SPECIAL

ALL I WANT IS SOMETHING …

GOCHUJANG BUTTER STEAK

I'm not really a big steak or beef eater at all, so when I do have it I want it to be very special. While chips are great, and are the classic pairing for steak, I don't think they really cut it – are they going to soak up all those delicious steak juices and butter? No, I don't think so, and this is why I think we should all be eating our steaks with rice. Once you try it I know you will be convinced. My spicy umami gochujang butter and steak juices perfectly smother the short-grain rice, for a really special steak dinner (you can even have some chips on the side if you really must!).

2 rib-eye steaks, 200g each and about 2cm thick

200g short-grain rice

2 cloves of garlic, unpeeled

vegetable oil

1 tbsp butter

salt

FOR THE GOCHUJANG BUTTER

50g salted butter, room temperature

1 tbsp (25g) gochujang

2 tbsp fresh coriander, finely chopped

1 clove of garlic, grated

1 tbsp soy sauce

½ tsp crispy chilli oil

a pinch of flaky sea salt

½ tsp honey

Heavily salt the steaks and allow them to sit for about 30 minutes at room temperature or up to overnight in the fridge. If you don't have at least 30 minutes, just salt them right before cooking.

Rinse the rice in cold water three times, until the water is almost clear. Alternatively, soak the rice for 30 minutes.

Drain the rice and put into a pan with 250ml of water. Bring to the boil, then turn the heat to low and allow to cook with the lid on for 12 minutes. Turn off the heat and allow to rest for 10 minutes with the lid on.

Beat the ingredients for the gochujang butter in a bowl – if your butter isn't at room temperature, use an electric whisk. Lay out a large piece of cling film and spoon the butter into the middle. Roll up the cling film to form a butter log and twist the ends. Place in the freezer for 10 minutes, just to firm up slightly, you don't want it frozen. Or, if you're feeling cheffy, you could also try quenelling the butter for an extra fancy finish.

Crush the garlic, keeping the skins on.

Heat a few tablespoons of oil in a cast-iron pan on the highest heat until smoking. Add the steaks and cook for 3 minutes on one side (this will be roughly 4 minutes in total for rare, 5–6 minutes in total for medium and 8–10 minutes for well done). Once you have flipped the steak once, and it's nicely seared on both sides, add 1 tablespoon of butter and the crushed garlic cloves. Baste the steak with the butter for 2 minutes.

Remove the steak from the pan and allow to rest for 5 minutes. Slice into strips, against the grain, and serve on top of the rice. Top with a slice of gochujang butter and allow it to melt slightly, then drizzle with any remaining resting juices.

LEFTOVERS
→   If you have extra gochujang butter, store it in the fridge and use it to cook up some eggs or to slather over a cheese toastie! Even with some rice and a fried egg!

SPECIAL

ALL I WANT IS SOMETHING …

ALL I WANT IS …

SOMETHING SWEET

THE BROWNIE RECIPE

This may be my most prized recipe, and I am gifting it to you in my book. When I so tragically got fired from my job in the midst of Covid, my friend convinced me to start selling brownies to make some money. I spent months developing the recipe, trying every brownie hack you have ever come across on the internet, getting feedback from Google Forms to make them better, even getting boxes designed so I could ship them across the country. We were selling hundreds of boxes a week, all being sold out in a matter of minutes and made by me and my mum in our tiny kitchen in Slough. I don't think I'll be selling them again any time soon, so for now you can use this recipe to make them at home.

250g dark chocolate

200g soft dark brown sugar   ↔ soft light brown sugar

200g butter

75g plain flour

50g cornflour

25g cocoa powder

5g baking powder

½ teaspoon salt

50g white chocolate

4 eggs

Preheat the oven to 160°C, and line a 20cm square cake tin with baking paper.

Melt 200g of dark chocolate in the microwave, 30 seconds at a time and stirring in between.

Beat the sugar and butter together for 10 minutes using an electric beater – the butter will turn a very pale colour.

Meanwhile, sift together the plain flour, cornflour, cocoa powder, baking powder and salt.

Roughly chop the remaining dark chocolate and the white chocolate into irregular-sized chunks.

Add the eggs to the sugar and butter one by one.

Drizzle in the melted chocolate in a stream on the side while still mixing the eggs, making sure the chocolate has cooled.

Add the flour mix and mix well until just combined, then stir in three-quarters of the chopped chocolate.

Pour this into the prepared tray and sprinkle with the rest of the chopped chocolate.

Bake for 13 minutes, then remove from the oven and tap firmly against the countertop. Allow to cool for 20 minutes. Bake again for 13–15 minutes – it will still be very soft and have a light jiggle. A toothpick should come out with moist crumbs, neither totally sticky or clean. Careful not to hit a melted chocolate puddle (I would insert two toothpicks at different points to be certain!).

Allow to cool fully and refrigerate for at least 4 hours to set.

Slice into pieces and serve.

NOTE

→   These are cooked quite low and slow to make them extra fudgy. I also found leaving them out for 15 minutes mid-cook creates the most delicious melt-in-the-mouth texture.

SWEET

ALL I WANT IS SOMETHING...

TIME (DOUGHNUTS)
30 MINUTES
+ 2–3 HOURS PROVING

TIME (FILLING)
PISTACHIO 20 MINUTES
TANGFASTIC 10 MINUTES

MAKES
8 DOUGHNUTS

DOUGHNUTS TWO-WAYS

There really is nothing like a homemade doughnut. Trust me, when you make them at home and realize how easy they are, you will put every single bakery doughnut to shame. They really do taste the best within three hours of making, so keep that in mind.

I've given you two filling options here, both equally easy.

First up, a game-changing hack – melting down a high-quality pistachio ice cream. Why start from scratch when someone has already done the hard work for you? Pistachio butter is a pain to find, and don't even get me started on making your own. Let the ice cream do the heavy lifting and enjoy the pistachio bliss.

The second is as if a custard doughnut and the red crocodile Tangfastic had a baby. I had this idea because the sugar lips you get from traditional doughnuts reminded me of the same feeling you get from Tangfastics. It's sweet but sour, creamy, and it balances all the richness from the doughnut.

FOR THE DOUGH

150ml whole milk

30g caster sugar

7g dried active yeast

250g strong white bread flour

a pinch of salt

1 egg, beaten

50g softened butter

vegetable oil

For the pistachio ice cream filling

500ml pistachio ice cream

50g cornflour

1 tbsp pistachio paste   ⸺ optional

200ml double cream

2 tbsp white sugar

FOR THE TANGFASTIC FILLING

300ml double cream

75g white sugar

150g strawberry   ↔ your favourite jam
or raspberry jam

2 tsp citric acid

NOTES

→   *Don't worry too much if your ice cream pint isn't exactly 500g – anywhere between 450g and 500g will do!*

→   *If you can get hold of it, try using pistachio kulfi instead of traditional ice cream.*

→   *Fill the doughnuts when you are ready to serve. They will stay fresh in an airtight container for 1 day, but they are best filled and eaten on the day!*

SWEET

ALL I WANT IS SOMETHING …

DOUGH

Warm the milk and sugar in a saucepan until the mixture is just lukewarm – test this with your finger, it should be just warm to the touch. Stir in the yeast and allow it to sit for 5–10 minutes, until it starts to foam slightly. This will let you know if your yeast is still alive.

In a stand mixer fitted with a dough hook, combine the flour and a pinch of salt. Add the yeasty milk and the egg and mix on a medium speed for 5 minutes, until the dough comes away from the side of the bowl. Cover the bowl with a clean tea towel or cling film and allow it to relax for 5 minutes.

Run your stand mixer again on a medium-high speed and spoon in 1 teaspoon of butter at a time until it's been absorbed into the dough. Your butter must be soft enough to push your finger through, otherwise it won't combine with the dough.

Knead the dough in the mixer for 8 minutes on a medium speed, to form a smooth and shiny dough. It will still be very sticky.

Cover the bowl with a kitchen towel and allow the dough to rise until doubled in size. This could take anything from 1 to 2 hours.

Punch the dough to release all the air and pull out large tangerine-sized balls (roughly 60g). Flatten each ball on a lightly floured work surface and fold the outsides into the middle. Turn the ball over and roll it into a smooth ball with your hands.

Cut out 8 squares of baking paper, around 10 x 10 cms. Transfer the dough balls to a baking sheet, putting each ball on a square of baking paper. Cover with cling film and allow to rise until doubled in size. This should take about 30 minutes. When proven correctly, they will spring back halfway when you gently press the side with your index finger.

Meanwhile, heat a large pan of oil, using a thermometer – the sweet spot is 165°C, so try to adjust the heat levels to stick to that number.

Fry your doughnuts in the hot oil, leaving the baking paper on and removing it once it's released into the oil. Cook on both sides for 2 minutes, until golden brown. If you see a white ring (i.e. the white ring of confidence), your doughnuts will be light and airy!

Allow to cool for 15–20 minutes before filling.

PISTACHIO ICE CREAM FILLING

Put the ice cream into a pan and melt it down (sacrilege, I know, but it will be fine, just keep going).

Meanwhile, mix the cornflour with 5 tablespoons of water. Add to the melted ice cream and whisk together. Turn the heat to low and continue whisking for 6–8 minutes, until the mixture is very thick.

Pour on to a flat plate and cover with cling film, so it touches the ice cream. Allow to chill fully in the fridge.

When ready to serve, whip the double cream to form medium peaks. Add a large spoon of the cream into the ice cream paste and mix well with a whisk to lighten the base. Then fold in the rest with a spatula.

Put the filling into a piping bag with a nozzle (any shape nozzle will work as long as it is big enough). Use a knife to make a hole in the side of each doughnut and pipe the filling into the hole until the doughnut feels heavy.

Toss the filled doughnut in white sugar and serve immediately.

TANGFASTIC FILLING

Whip the cream with 1 tablespoon of white sugar until it forms stiff peaks.

Fill one piping bag with a nozzle (any shape) with the cream and another with the jam.

Use a knife to make a hole in the side of each doughnut and pipe in 2 tablespoons of jam filling. Then pipe in the cream.

Combine the remaining sugar and citric acid in a bowl and toss the filled doughnuts. Serve immediately.

UPSIDE-DOWN RASPBERRY, ORANGE & OLIVE OIL CAKE

Upside-down cakes are one of the best baking hacks around. Carefully placing fresh and beautiful fruit at the bottom makes a glorious cake top that needs no decorating but looks incredibly impressive. Here, I've combined my favourite lemon and poppy seed cake with fresh tart raspberries.

350g raspberries

250g white sugar, plus 3 tbsp

2 oranges, zested

250g thick Greek yoghurt (must be full-fat)

3 large eggs

150g extra virgin olive oil

¼ tsp salt

1 tbsp black poppy seeds

200g plain flour

½ tsp baking powder

½ tsp bicarbonate of soda

Preheat the oven to 180°C.

Line a 20cm cake tin with baking paper. Gently press in the raspberries, top side down (so the hole is facing upwards), to cover the entire bottom surface of the cake tin. Sprinkle with 3 tablespoons of sugar and set aside.

Tip the rest of the sugar into a large bowl and zest in the oranges. Rub the sugar and zest together with your fingers.

Add the yoghurt, eggs, oil, salt and poppy seeds and mix well.

Sift in the flour, baking powder and bicarb and mix to form a smooth batter.

Carefully pour the batter over the raspberries and bake for 40–45 minutes, until a toothpick comes out clean.

SWEET

199

ALL I WANT IS SOMETHING …

FUDGY BANANA BARS

I've had enough of banana bread. We all have made enough banana bread, but I can never seem to use up all my bananas. So I developed these super-decadent bars, which feel like the lovechild of fudgy brownies and banana bread. Thanks to a little cornflour magic, a technique which I've learnt making mochi traditionally using glutinous rice flour, the texture totally transforms as it cools. Make sure to try a piece straight out of the oven for a gooey, warm bite, and then again when it's cooled for a chewy fudgy version – both with a generous glass of cold milk!

175g butter

3 brown bananas

200g condensed milk

3 eggs

200g dark brown sugar

100g plain flour

50g cornflour

½ tsp salt

½ tsp baking powder

FOR THE FROSTING

brown butter solids (see method)

150g cream cheese

2 tbsp condensed milk

1 tsp ground cinnamon

Preheat the oven to 170°C. Butter and flour a 23cm square tin and line it with baking paper.

Melt the butter in a saucepan and cook for 15 minutes on a low-medium heat, until it has browned and smells nutty. It will start getting foamy at first, and then it will turn a nutty brown with dark solids at the bottom. Strain the butter, reserving the dark solids for later.

Mash the bananas with the condensed milk. Use a hand blender to make this mixture smooth if you don't want chunks of banana in your bars. Add the melted brown butter, eggs, sugar, plain flour, cornflour, salt and baking powder. Mix well until smooth.

Pour into the prepared tin and bake for 25 minutes (a toothpick should come out sticky).

For best results allow to cool for 12 hours, refrigerated. Try a piece straight out of the oven and then watch the texture transform over time.

For the frosting, whip the saved brown butter solids with the cream cheese and condensed milk.

Cut the banana bars into squares and spread over the frosting. Sprinkle over a pinch of cinnamon and enjoy.

NOTES

→   If you don't have any brown bananas and you can't wait, put your bananas into the oven for 15 minutes at 200°C.

→   Try adding chopped nuts, chocolate or dried fruit. You can even add spices such as cinnamon or nutmeg to the batter!

→   Save the rest of your condensed milk in an airtight jar in the fridge. It will keep for months and is great for sweetening tea and coffee.

SWEET

ALL I WANT IS SOMETHING …

WHITE CHOCOLATE & MANDARIN BURNT BASQUE CHEESECAKE

I normally can't stand cheesecake – it always feels too heavy and stodgy. But when I tried a burnt Basque cheesecake for the first time, my mind was blown. It's like a combination of a custard and a cheesecake, where the inside is majorly creamy. And it's probably the easiest dessert you can make.

Mandarin and white chocolate hold a very special place in my heart, and it all began in a quaint ice cream shop nestled in the Isle of Wight, a place named Crave. Their best-selling ice cream was mandarin and white chocolate. It was remarkably creamy and rich, with thick Cornish cream, white chocolate and vibrant bursts of mandarin. But the best part was Tracy and Chris, who spent their summers orchestrating wild and imaginative ice cream flavours such as mango sticky rice and lemon pancake. They would use this ice cream money to spend their winters travelling through the sunniest parts of the world, finding inspiration for their next ice cream flavour. And I think that's actually all I want in life too.

200g white chocolate, roughly chopped

200g caster sugar

6 mandarins (easy peelers)

1kg cream cheese

¼ tsp salt

200g thick Greek yoghurt

6 eggs

40g plain flour

2 tbsp white sugar

Preheat the oven to 250°C.

Lay a very large piece of baking paper over a 23cm cake tin. Push the paper inwards so it covers the whole inside of the tin. If your baking paper is not big enough, use two sheets, making sure they overlap in the middle.

Put the white chocolate into a microwave-safe bowl and melt it in the microwave 30 seconds at a time, stirring in between.

Place the sugar in a large bowl and zest 4 of the mandarins over the top. Rub the sugar and zest together until the sugar is orange – this releases the oils in the zest, making it more flavourful. Add the cream cheese, salt and yoghurt, and beat until very smooth. Add the eggs one at a time, beating between each edition.

Pour in the cooled white chocolate and stir. Remove about 1 cup of the mixture and put it into another bowl, then whisk the flour into this second bowl until smooth. Add back to the cheesecake mix.

Pour the batter into the prepared tin and bake in the oven for 27–30 minutes. The cheesecake will be very soft and wobbly, and the top will be dark, but don't worry – this is what will make it super-luscious and creamy. Allow to cool to room temperature on the counter, then refrigerate overnight.

Peel the 4 zested mandarins, scrape off any pith and break into segments. Juice the remaining 2 mandarins. Combine the juice with the sugar and microwave for 30 seconds. Add the peeled mandarin segments and mix, then top the cheesecake.

NOTE

→   You can sub in any other citrus fruit you like – try grapefruit, or lemon with some lemon curd over the top.

CHOCOLATEY PEANUT BUTTER CARAMEL TART

This recipe honours one of my favourite chocolates, Reese's peanut butter cups. It's the dessert I made most often when I was at university, because all my friends raved on about it so much, and because it tastes like a more luscious giant Reese's cupcake. The filling is a really simple peanut butter caramel, smooth and gooey, encased in a salty savoury pretzel crust.

FOR THE BASE

300g pretzels	↔ digestive biscuits

200g butter

4 tbsp water

FOR THE PEANUT BUTTER FILLING

200g crunchy peanut butter

300ml double cream

150g light brown sugar

salt

FOR THE CHOCOLATE TOPPING

200g dark chocolate, broken into pieces

300ml double cream

FOR THE CRUNCHY TOPPING

2 tbsp pretzels

2 tbsp salted, roasted peanuts

50g Reese's Pieces, chopped

a pinch of flaky sea salt

Preheat the oven to 180°C.

Blitz the pretzels to a fine powder. Melt the butter in the microwave and add to the pretzels along with the water. Combine until the mixture resembles wet sand.

Pour half the pretzel mix into a 23cm deep tart tin and press it out to the edges with your hands. Tip in the remaining pretzel mix and press down to make the base. Use the back of a spoon or cup to help you press it down.

Place on a baking tray and bake in the oven for 15 minutes.

Meanwhile, put the peanut butter, cream and light brown sugar into a small pan and bring to a simmer. Allow to bubble for 10 minutes on a low heat, until very thick, stirring constantly. Scrape to the bottom as it can catch easily. Finish with a pinch of salt (if your peanut butter is unsalted).

Pour the peanut caramel over the base and allow to cool slightly.

Put the chocolate into a bowl, and heat up the double cream. Pour the hot cream over the chocolate and allow to sit for 5 minutes. Stir together until it has all melted, then pour over the peanut caramel layer.

For the topping, lightly crush the remaining pretzels, peanuts, Reese's Pieces and salt and sprinkle them on top of the tart.

Allow to cool in the fridge before serving.

NOTE

→ *Use whatever chocolate is your favourite for the topping, if you like a specific brand or percentage. I love how the dark chocolate cuts through the rich filling, but if you prefer milk chocolate, use that.*

SWEET

ALL I WANT IS SOMETHING …

COCONUT CREAM KEY LIME PIE

One thing that has always had space in my brain is the coconut cream pie from that *iCarly* episode, the one where we were driven to the brink of pie-induced madness. Now, here's the thing: I never considered myself a coconut enthusiast, until I recreated it with homemade coconut cream and flakes and tasted this pie of dreams.

     This pie is a simpler but more balanced version, with a thick layer of zesty key lime – another childhood classic of mine, and my brother's favourite dessert.

175g digestive biscuits

75g desiccated coconut, plus 2 tbsp for decorating

100g butter

1 x 400g tin of sweetened condensed milk

100ml lime juice (from about 4 limes)

zest of 4 limes

100g yoghurt

400ml coconut milk

200g creamed coconut (block)

150g granulated sugar

2 tbsp cornflour

300ml double cream

½ tsp salt

Preheat the oven to 180°C.

     Blitz the digestive biscuits with the desiccated coconut to form a fine crumb.

     Melt the butter and stir into the biscuit mix until it resembles wet sand.

     Pour the mix into a 20cm tart tin and press it down so it is evenly distributed along the edges and over the base. Use a small cup or spoon to help you press it.

     Bake in the oven for 10 minutes, or until lightly golden. Allow to cool fully.

     Meanwhile, mix together the condensed milk, lime juice, lime zest and yoghurt. Pour into the tart case and bake for 10 minutes, then remove and allow to cool completely.

     Heat the coconut milk, creamed coconut and sugar. Bring to a bubble and simmer for 15 minutes or until reduced by half.

     Mix the cornflour with 1 tablespoon of water and add to the coconut milk. Cook for another 5 minutes, until thickened. Pour on to a plate and cover with cling film so it touches the coconut, then put into the fridge or freezer to cool completely (fridge 4 hours, freezer 1 hour).

     Whisk the double cream to form stiff peaks and fold in the cooled coconut milk mixture. Stir in the ½ teaspoon of salt.

     Spread the cream over the chilled pie, creating texture with the back of a spoon.

     Toast the remaining 2 tablespoons of desiccated coconut in a dry pan for 3 minutes, until golden, and sprinkle over the top of the pie.

     You can keep the pie refrigerated for a day, but add the desiccated coconut when ready to serve, or serve it immediately.

NOTE

→   *If you must, you can add a tiny drop of green food colouring to the lime layer, but be careful not to add too much so that it looks like a Shrek pie.*

207

MASALA HOT CHOCO & CHURROS

Masala hot chocolate is a concoction I made in the depths of winter, when my mum would be making me endless cups of chai and I had so much chocolate left over from my brownie-making. It's warming, lightly spiced and so rich and creamy. Using a mix of real chocolate and cocoa powder is the trick to making it extra indulgent. And for the book I've made it into an all-round dessert by dunking in some crispy cinnamon churros for the perfect winter treat.

FOR THE HOT CHOCOLATE

4cm ginger

5 cardamom pods

½ tsp black peppercorns

1 cinnamon stick

200ml water

3 teabags

600ml milk

100g dark chocolate, chopped

1 tbsp cocoa powder

75g sugar

½ tsp salt

FOR THE CINNAMON CHURROS

150ml milk

100g unsalted butter

1 tbsp sugar

1 tsp salt

150g plain flour

3 large eggs

vegetable oil, for deep-frying

FOR THE SPICED SUGAR

4 tbsp white sugar

1 tsp ground cinnamon

½ tsp ground ginger

MASALA HOT CHOCO

Gently crush the whole spices and put them into to a pan with the water and the opened tea bags. Boil on a high heat for 10 minutes, then add the milk and boil for another 10 minutes.

Strain the tea, discarding the spices and tea leaves, and put the liquid back on the hob.

Add the dark chocolate, cocoa powder, sugar and salt. Simmer for 5 minutes, whisking well, until all the chocolate has melted.

Taste, in case you want a sweeter hot chocolate, and enjoy in your favourite mug.

CINNAMON CHURROS

Heat the milk, butter, sugar and salt in a pan on a low heat until the butter is melted.

Add in the plain flour and beat it with a wooden spoon for a few minutes until it forms a dough that doesn't stick to the edges of the pan.

Take it off the heat and transfer the dough to a bowl. Crack in the eggs one at a time, beating very well after each addition. The dough will be smooth and glossy.

Transfer the dough to a piping bag with a star nozzle – you can also use a ziplock bag with a hole cut out of the corner!

Mix the spiced sugar ingredients together in a small bowl.

Heat up enough oil for deep frying, and heat to a medium heat.

Pipe the churros into the hot oil, snipping off the end with scissors. Pipe 3 or 4 at a time and allow them to cook for a few minutes on each side until the churros are crispy and golden.

Transfer to a plate lined with kitchen paper and dust with the spiced sugar.

SPICED RUM STICKY TOFFEE PUDDING

Sticky toffee pudding was always a household favourite – it's the first dessert I made successfully. I actually tested it for years, trying to get the perfect light fluffy sponge with sweet creamy caramel sauce that tastes like melted Werthers originals, but was also not too sweet. There was a moment where I had to put in a ban because my mum was requesting it so much!

The light fluffy sponge here has been infused with the flavours of black Jamaican rum cake. I don't often call for alcohol in my desserts, and this may be the only one I've had where the rum really complements the warmth of the spices and dark sugars.

250g whole medjool dates
(approx. 16–18 dates, weighed with seeds)

3 tsp bicarbonate of soda

1 tsp ground cinnamon

1 tsp grated ginger

100ml dark rum,   ↔ water
plus more for serving

85g butter, softened

200g dark brown sugar

2 eggs

2 tbsp black treacle   ↔ honey or golden syrup
(molasses)

100ml milk

175g plain flour

½ tsp salt

1 tsp baking powder

FOR THE TOFFEE SAUCE

100g butter, cut into pieces

200g dark brown sugar

300ml double cream

½ tsp salt

TO SERVE

vanilla ice cream

cream   ↔ custard

50g butter, to reheat   ⌣ optional

Preheat the oven to 180°C. Grease and line a 900g loaf tin.

Remove the stones from the dates, roughly chop, and put into a pan with 150ml of water and 1 teaspoon of bicarb, cinnamon and ginger. Cook for 10 minutes, pushing the dates down to form a thick paste. Remove from the heat and mix in the rum.

In a large bowl, beat the butter and brown sugar until fluffy. Add the eggs, date paste, molasses, milk and mix well. Add in the plain flour, 2 teaspoons of bicarb, salt and the baking powder and mix until just combined.

Pour into the prepared tin and bake for 50 minutes until a toothpick comes out with moist crumbs.

Meanwhile, make the toffee sauce. Melt the butter in a saucepan and add the brown sugar. Cook for 10 minutes, until bubbling rapidly, then add the double cream. Cook for another 2 minutes and add the ½ teaspoon of salt.

To serve, you can slice the cake and serve it hot with a scoop of ice cream, or cream, and lots of toffee sauce.

If the cake has been fully cooled, toast the slices with some butter in a pan on both sides, then top with ice cream and toffee sauce.

For some drama, pour 2 tablespoons of rum over the top of the cake and flambé with a blowtorch.

NOTES

→   *I've made this in a loaf tin because I like how easy it is to serve for a big crowd, but you could make it in a 25cm cake tin and check it in the oven after 35 minutes.*

CARAMELIZED BANANA SPLIT WITH HAZELNUT CHOCOLATE FUDGE

Banana splits have newly become my favourite desserts. They look super-impressive but are basically no work to make. And honestly, I feel like we often forget about them, so this is your reminder to make yourself one. A few shop-bought ingredients, some sprinkles, a cherry and you end up with a really show-stopping dessert fit for everyone.

3 tbsp double cream

3 tbsp Nutella

a pinch of salt

1 banana

2 tbsp white sugar

3 scoops of your favourite ice cream

1 can of squirty cream

2 tbsp sprinkles

3 glacé cherries

Put the double cream and Nutella into a microwave-safe bowl and melt in the microwave for 1 minute. Stir well to create a smooth sauce. Add a pinch of salt and mix again.

Peel the banana and slice in half lengthways. Sprinkle with sugar, then caramelize the sugar using a blowtorch. Alternatively, place under a very hot grill for 5 minutes, until the sugar is melted and caramelized.

Place your banana on a plate, and top with 3 scoops of your favourite ice cream. Drizzle with the chocolate sauce and squirt the cream on top. Decorate with the sprinkles and finish with the glacé cherries.

SWEET

ALL I WANT IS SOMETHING …

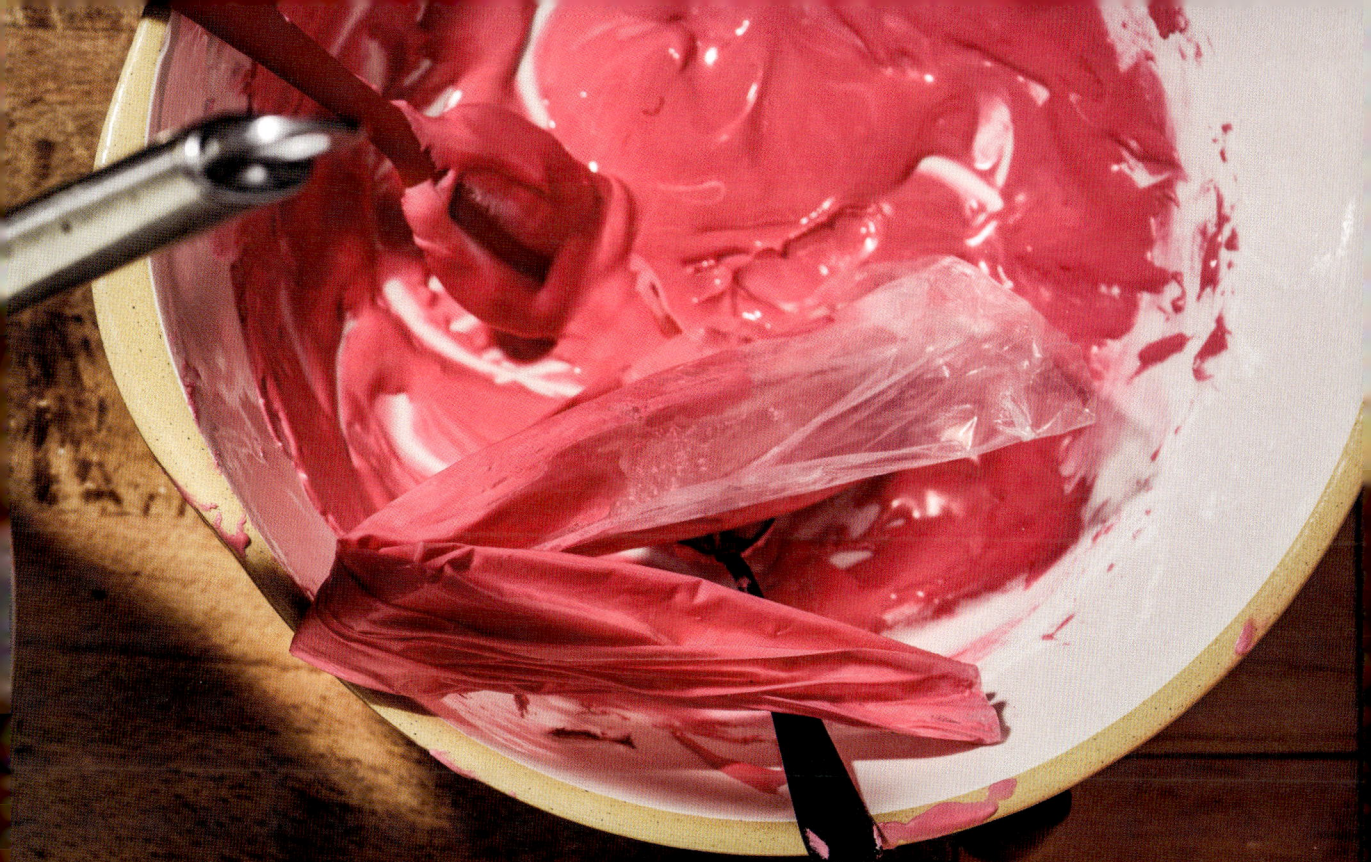

EMERGENCY BIRTHDAY CAKE

I've always believed that any occasion can become a celebration if you have a cake. New job, passing a test, learning to ride a bike . . . This is an emergency birthday cake, but it really can be used for any occasion, and is perfect for making someone feel incredibly special for very little effort. How did you feel last time someone made you a cake?

And before the purists come for me, think of this as a combination of a Japanese fruit sando (white bread with cream and fruit in a sandwich) and a Latin American tres leches cake (a very simple cake drenched in sweetened milk and topped with cream), combined with the assembly of a Swedish *smorgastorta*. It's one of my proudest creations to date and I even made it for my brother's engagement party.

3 tbsp condensed milk

4 tbsp milk

½ tsp vanilla extract

200g strawberries

12 slices of thick white bread
(usually one loaf is enough)

100g jam   ↔ any sweet sandwich filling (Nutella, Biscoff, marmalade)

FOR THE FILLING AND FROSTING

1200ml double cream

4 tbsp icing sugar

1 tsp vanilla extract

FOR DECORATING

50g sprinkles

1 tube of writing icing

Whip the double cream with the icing sugar and vanilla using an electric hand whisk (or a regular whisk and some elbow grease), until it's thick and stiff enough to stand up on its own.

Combine the condensed milk, milk and vanilla extract.

Slice the strawberries in half.

Cut the crusts off the bread and discard (or blitz them up and save them as breadcrumbs).

Lay out 4 slices of bread on your board to make a base, and 'glue' these down with a small amount of whipped cream.

Liberally brush the bread with half the condensed milk mixture, making sure to get right to the edges.

Spread 3 tablespoons of jam on the bread, then add half the sliced strawberries and finally a thick layer of cream.

Top with 4 more slices of bread and repeat, finishing with a layer of bread.

Cover the entire cake with whipped cream. If you like, you can pipe some of the cream in swirls on top, using a piping bag. Apply the sprinkles to the side of the cake and use writing icing to add a personalized message.

NOTES

→   *Use a brioche loaf for a more luxurious cake. You can even use a brioche burger bun to make a tiny lunchbox cake! Please do not use sourdough – the cheaper the white bread the better.*

→   *This is incredibly customizable – switch up the fruit, the jam, use chocolate frosting if you wish. I've created a super simple base so you can enjoy the creative process!*

ALL I WANT IS …

SOMETHING NOW!

EMERGENCY DUMPLING SOUP

Soups are my go-to when I'm feeling under the weather or nursing a hangover. And I always make sure to keep my freezer stocked with dumplings in cases like these. One day, after a particularly brutal hangover, I decided to combine the two, and it's been my soul-saving secret ever since. The magic ingredient is a whisked egg, which adds a delightful richness and velvetiness and just the right amount of thickness to the broth.

1 vegetable stock cube   ↔ chicken stock cube

7–10 frozen dumplings

1 tbsp soy sauce

1 tbsp Chinese black vinegar   ↔ balsamic vinegar

1 tsp crispy chilli oil

3 spring onions

1 egg

1 tsp sesame seeds   ⁓ optional

Start by bringing 500ml of water to a simmer in a pan. Crumble in the stock cube and toss in your dumplings.

Add the soy sauce, vinegar and chilli oil, and let it all boil away for 3 minutes (or according to the instructions on your dumpling packet).

Meanwhile, finely chop the spring onions. (For an easier option, you can use scissors and snip them directly over the soup bowl, to save the hassle of getting a cutting board and knife out.)

Crack the egg into the pan and give it a good whisk to create light, feathery strands.

Pour your delicious soup into a bowl and top it off with spring onions and a sprinkle of sesame seeds, if you like.

NOW!

NOTE

→   The beauty of this recipe lies in its versatility. You can toss in whatever you have lying around for extra flavour and goodness. I love adding chopped cabbage or some noodles for extra carbs. It's all about making it your own.

ALL I WANT IS SOMETHING …

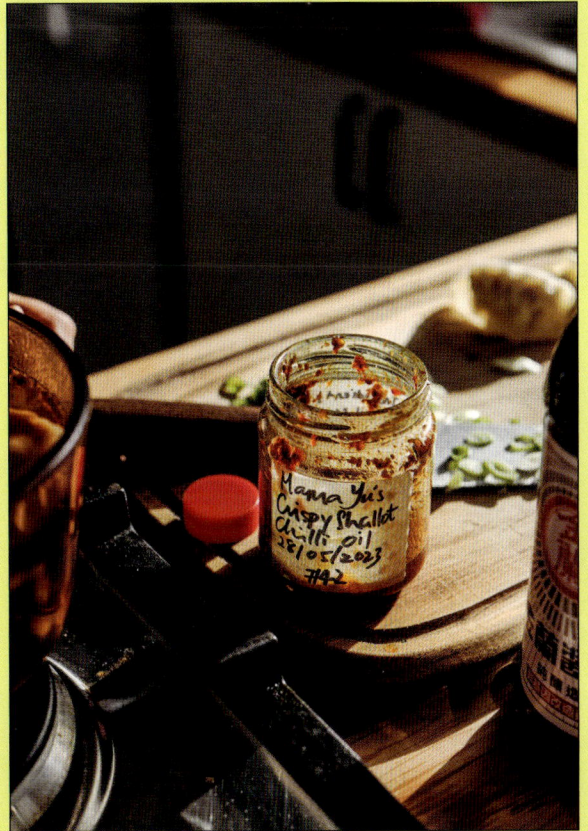

TIME
15 MINUTES

SERVES
2

VEGGIE (WITH SUBS)

15-MINUTE LAKSA

The times when I don't feel like cooking are usually the times I need something warming and spicy to wake myself up. I usually have a tub of Thai curry paste in the back of the fridge, which is perfect for a really speedy laksa that tastes like you spent hours on it.

Throw in whatever green veg you like, or even some prawns or tofu for extra protein!

2 eggs

1–2 tbsp Thai red curry paste
(depending on how spicy your paste is)

400ml coconut milk

1 tbsp fish sauce   ↔ veggie fish sauce

1 tbsp soy sauce

½ tsp sugar

200g instant ramen noodles (two packs)

any green veg (bok choy, sugar snap peas, asparagus, spinach)

vegetable oil

TO SERVE

spring onions, chopped

NOW!

Bring a pan of water to the boil and cook your eggs for 6 minutes. Remove the eggs but keep the boiling water.

Heat a glug of oil in a pan and add the curry paste. Cook for 2 minutes, then add the coconut milk, fish sauce, soy sauce and sugar. Add 500ml of water and season to taste.

Use the hot water to cook the noodles, according to the packet instructions, and the green veg (they should cook for roughly the same time).

Divide the noodles and veg between two bowls. Pour over the laksa and top with a boiled egg each, cut in half. Top with the chopped spring onions.

NOTES
→ *If you're vegetarian, always check the ingredients on your curry paste to ensure that it doesn't contain fish sauce or shrimp paste.*

SOPHIE'S CHORIZO & CHICKPEA STEW

My friend Sophie KT once told me about her emergency meal and I could not stop thinking about it. Here is her iconic chorizo and chickpea stew, which takes only 15 minutes and has five main ingredients. It really couldn't be any simpler. I've even used it as inspo for my chorizo and pea pozole (page 74), if you want to make something similar and have a little more time. So this is from her emergency kitchen to yours.

200g chorizo

4 cloves of garlic

1 x 400g tin of chickpeas

1 tsp smoked paprika

1 tsp dried oregano

½ tsp salt

olive oil

Roughly chop the chorizo and garlic. Toss into a pan with a big glug of oil on a high heat and sear for 5 minutes, until the oil is red and the chorizo starts to crisp up. Pour in the chickpeas with their liquid and 300ml water, along with the smoked paprika and oregano.

Bring to a simmer and season with salt. You can smash some of the chickpeas against the side of the pan if you like, to thicken the stew slightly.

Serve as is, or with some crusty bread.

NOTE

→ Swap out any beans you have! Throw in some potatoes or other veggies if you have a little more time.

NOW!

ALL I WANT IS SOMETHING …

SPICY GARLICKY SOY SAUCE PASTA

Spaghetti aglio e olio – it's been the go-to quick-fix meal for countless folks for decades. Legend has it that even Italians whip it up after a night out (and half drunk) because it's just that easy to throw together. The core of this pasta dish remains true to its roots, but we're spicing it up with a few Chinese ingredients. The real star here is the crispy chilli oil, a pantry essential (or it should be). Feel free to choose your favourite brand and adjust the heat level to your liking by controlling the chilli bits.

200g spaghetti

10 cloves of garlic, thinly sliced

2 tbsp chilli oil

1 tsp grated ginger

3 spring onions, thinly sliced

2 tbsp chilli oil bits

2–3 tbsp soy sauce

50g Parmesan, grated, plus extra to serve ↔ veggie Parmesan or other hard cheese

a small handful of fresh coriander, finely chopped

salt

Cook the spaghetti in lightly salted boiling water for about 10 minutes, until al dente.

Meanwhile, in a large pan, cook the garlic in the chilli oil over the lowest heat possible for about 4–5 minutes, until it's really soft.

Add the ginger, spring onions and chilli oil bits, then continue cooking on a low heat until the pasta is ready (about 5 minutes).

Transfer the cooked spaghetti to the aromatic mixture using tongs, ensuring you don't fully drain the pasta. Pour in 150ml of the pasta cooking water.

Turn up the heat to medium and stir well, so the pasta absorbs most of the water. If it looks too dry, add more water in small amounts until the pasta is well coated.

Add 2 tablespoons of soy sauce and the Parmesan, taste, and add more soy sauce if needed.

Stir in the coriander, grate over the extra Parmesan, and serve.

NOTE

→   For this dish, I keep the pasta lightly salted to allow room for a generous splash of soy sauce and a generous sprinkle of Parmesan without turning it into a salty whirlwind. Try to use as little water as possible for cooking the pasta – this means the water will be extra starchy, resulting in a super-glossy sauce.

NOW!

CHEAT'S DORITOS CHILAQUILES

This is basically how to turn a bag of tortilla chips from the night before into a meal.
It's inspired by a Mexican classic, traditionally made to use up old and stale tortilla chips,
but in my experience it is fantastic with a bag of Doritos.

1 large tomato

2 cloves of garlic

1 chilli   ↔ ½ tsp chilli powder

½ tsp dried oregano

1 bag of Doritos (70g)   ↔ any other tortilla chips

2 tbsp Cheddar cheese, grated, plus extra to serve

1 egg

1 tbsp sour cream   ↔ yoghurt

hot sauce (I like El Yucateco or Cholula)

vegetable oil

salt

NOW!

Blitz up the tomato, garlic, chilli, oregano and ¼ teaspoon of salt in a blender.

Heat a glug of oil in a pan and cook the tomato mixture for 5 minutes on a high heat, until it starts to become a thick sauce. Season with a pinch of salt and add the Doritos and the grated cheese. Mix well and cook for 1 minute, so that the crisps are coated in the sauce but still slightly crispy.

Transfer to a serving plate and then add a glug of oil to the same pan and fry an egg until crispy.

Top with the fried egg, more grated cheese, the sour cream and some hot sauce.

NOTE

→   *Regular crisps don't work here, they must be corn tortilla chips, but any brand will do! Please don't use salt and vinegar crisps.*

CHEESY GOCHUJANG TORTELLINI

I think we can agree that premade tortellini is the universal knight in shining armour for uni students everywhere. They are sold in almost every corner shop, and these little pasta pockets promise a satisfying meal in less than 10 minutes. Now imagine them flavoured like Korean tteokbokki – a marvellous dish using chewy rice cakes in a spicy sweet gochujang sauce. These rice cakes can be a bit tricky to source, so this recipe lets you have all the fun of the flavours without driving for hours.

½ an onion, sliced

1 clove of garlic, grated

1 tbsp gochujang

1 tbsp soy sauce

150g cheese tortellini

1 spring onion, chopped into 3cm pieces

vegetable oil

EXTRAS

1 tbsp crispy chilli oil

½ tsp sesame seeds

grated Cheddar cheese

In a frying pan, fry the onion and garlic in a glug of oil for 2 minutes.

Whisk together the gochujang, soy sauce and 200ml of water. Add this to the pan along with the tortellini and the spring onions. Bring to a bubble and cook for 6–7 minutes, until the tortellini are soft and cooked through.

Top with the crispy chilli oil, sesame seeds and a scattering of grated Cheddar cheese.

NOW!

NOTE
→ *I used cheese tortellini because gochujang and cheese are a fantastic combo, but play around with the other flavours you can find – just avoid things like pesto!*

233

ALL I WANT IS SOMETHING …

SPICY TUNA RICE BOWL

All of us have a tin of tuna lying around at the back of the cupboard, and paired with some hot rice, it makes a pretty great meal in less than 10 minutes – it tastes kind of like a spicy tuna roll if you squint.

100g cooked rice

1 x 150g tin of tuna, drained

2 tbsp mayonnaise

2 tbsp sriracha   ← chilli oil, or my fave, both!

1 tbsp soy sauce

1 tsp lime juice   ← rice vinegar

1 spring onion, chopped, to serve

Heat the cooked rice in the microwave for 1 minute. Transfer it to a bowl.

Scoop out the tuna from the tin and place on top of the rice.

Spoon over the mayo, sriracha or chilli oil, soy sauce and lime juice or vinegar.

Sprinkle with spring onions, mix together and enjoy.

NOTES

→   Use packet microwave rice at a pinch, it's an emergency after all.

→   Other topping ideas: fried egg, butter, sesame seeds, crispy onions, black vinegar.

ALL I WANT IS SOMETHING …

NOW!

BURSTING CHERRY TOMATO & HARISSA PASTA

This pasta brings together fresh cherry tomatoes and the spicy richness of harissa, complemented by a luscious egg yolk. It's a speedy pasta dish that effortlessly satisfies all your cravings.

150g penne	
3 cloves of garlic, chopped	
150g cherry tomatoes, halved	
1–2 tbsp harissa	↔ miso or anchovies
30g Parmesan cheese, grated, plus extra for serving	↔ veggie Parmesan or other hard cheese
1 egg yolk	↔ 3 tbsp cream
1 tsp freshly ground black pepper	
salt	
olive oil	

Cook the pasta in boiling salted water for 10 minutes or according to the packet instructions, until al dente, using less water than usual in order to make a starchier sauce.

Pour a large glug of olive oil into a pan and add the garlic, cherry tomatoes and the harissa. Cook on a high heat, smushing down the tomatoes until they are slightly blistered.

Drain the pasta, reserving the cooking water. Add the cooked pasta to the pan, along with a ladle of the cooking water. Toss very well and add the Parmesan.

Turn off the heat and add the egg yolk, tossing very well to create a glossy sauce.

Season generously with salt and pepper and serve with more grated Parmesan.

NOTES

→   When big tomatoes are your only option, grate them using a box grater, leaving the skin behind, and use the pulp for your sauce. You can even use half a tin of chopped tomatoes.

→   Try using sambal or Thai curry paste as a savoury alternative to harissa.

→   If you have some fresh basil or parsley, that would be great for adding freshness!

ALL I WANT IS SOMETHING …

NOW!

TOMATO & PEANUT UDON

Udon are fantastic noodles for when you're in a rush because they cook so fast, and this thick peanutty sauce is perfect with them. Inspired by one of my favourite national dishes, the Ghanaian groundnut soup, I've taken the flavours of spicy tomato and peanut, and it only takes a few more ingredients to make this taste great!

1 tbsp tomato purée

1 tbsp peanut butter

1 tsp chilli oil

¼ tsp salt

1 pack of udon noodles (single portion)

1 spring onion

a small handful of fresh coriander

½ a lime

vegetable oil

Heat up a glug of oil in a small pan and fry the tomato purée for 3 minutes until the colour darkens.

In a bowl, whisk the peanut butter with 200ml of water. Pour the peanut water into the pan of tomato purée, then add the chilli oil and salt, and whisk together.

Add the udon noodles and allow to bubble without stirring for 5 minutes, until the noodles loosen.

Meanwhile, chop the spring onions and coriander.

Once the udon noodles are cooked and the sauce is thick, transfer them to your plate, top with spring onions and coriander, and sprinkle over the juice of half a lime.

NOW!

NOTE

→   Don't skip the lime – it's essential for cutting through all the richness of the peanut butter. Switch out for a lemon if you must!

ALL I WANT IS SOMETHING …

MUM'S EMERGENCY 10-MINUTE DAL

This is my mum's original emergency recipe. Her friend was coming down with the flu, and she was craving my mum's dal. My mum offered to make her some but her friend was convinced it would take too long so they placed a bet. And my mum made dal and rice from scratch in under 10 minutes. And believe me, I've put her to the test, timing her over and over!

250g split red lentils

300g tinned chopped tomatoes

8cm ginger

8 cloves of garlic

½ tsp cumin seeds

½ tsp ground turmeric

1 tsp ground cumin

1 tsp ground coriander

2 tsp chilli powder

a small handful of fresh coriander, chopped

3 green chillies

3 sprigs of curry leaves — optional but highly recommended

vegetable oil

salt

Begin by putting the red lentils into a large pan and rinsing them with hot tap water at least three times, until the water runs almost clear. It's important that the water is warm; this helps the lentils cook faster. Drain the lentils, put them back into the pan and add 750ml of warm water. Bring to the boil, then boil for 7 minutes on a high heat.

While the lentils are cooking, use a handheld blender to blend the chopped tomatoes, half the ginger and 4 cloves of garlic.

Pour a good amount of vegetable oil into a large pan and add the cumin seeds. Wait for them to start sizzling and dancing around the pan, then carefully pour in the blended tomatoes. Add the turmeric, ground cumin, ground coriander, chilli powder and 2 teaspoons of salt, and cook on a medium heat for at least 7 minutes, or until the dal is fully cooked.

To check if the dal is ready, press a few of the lentils between your fingers to see if they are tender. Add the cooked dal with its liquid to the pan of curried tomatoes and mix well. If it's too thick, add 150ml more water to reach your desired consistency.

Taste for seasoning and stir in three-quarters of the chopped coriander.

In the meantime, thinly slice the remaining 4 cloves of garlic, halve the green chillies and cut the remaining ginger into matchsticks.

To make the tarka, heat 2 tablespoons of oil in a small pan and gently cook the garlic until it turns golden. Add the chillies and cook for 15 seconds, then add the curry leaves. Cook for about 10 seconds, until they turn bright green, then immediately pour this aromatic mix over the dal. Cover with a lid and let the flavours infuse until you're ready to eat.

Finish with the matchsticked ginger and the rest of the chopped coriander, and serve with fluffy basmati rice or homemade rotli (page 151).

NOTE

→ *Don't skip the tarka – this wonderfully aromatic and flavourful oil will make the dal into something really spectacular with almost no effort! It's a technique used in Indian cuisine, tempering herbs and spices to add layers of flavour to curries.*

NOW!

ALL I WANT IS SOMETHING …

INDEX